Pr.   Other

"*A Grief like No Other is a landmark contribution* to the field and should be read by all therapists and those touched by the violent loss of someone in their lives. This remarkable, beautifully written, yet practical guide evolved out of Kathleen's own horrendous loss of her son and her unremitting quest for knowledge, spirituality and transformation. She has transformed the unbearable pain in her life to understanding and peace and offers it to us who are searching for answers—and healing."

—Dr. Bonnie Kellen, PhD, clinical psychologist

"A book of comfort for losses that seem unfathomable, a hug of hope along a journey that seems impossible, a map of what lies ahead from a kindred spirit who knows every twist in the path."

—Rachel Simon, author of *Riding the Bus with My Sister*

Kathleen O'Hara, MA, is a therapist who received her BA from Antioch University and her graduate degree in psychology from the California Institute of Integral Studies. O'Hara lives in Philadelphia, where she maintains a private practice.

A Grief Like No Other

A Grief Like No Other

SURVIVING THE VIOLENT
DEATH OF SOMEONE YOU LOVE

Kathleen O'Hara, MA

MARLOWE & COMPANY
NEW YORK

A Grief Like No Other:
Surviving the Violent Death of Someone You Love

Copyright © 2006 by Kathleen O'Hara
Foreword copyright © 2006 by Dan Gottlieb, PhD

Published by
Marlowe & Company
An Imprint of Avalon Publishing Group, Incorporated
245 West 17th Street ✦ 11th Floor
New York, NY 10011-5300

AVALON
publishing group incorporated

Library of Congress Cataloging-in-Publication Data
O'Hara, Kathleen A., 1953–
A grief like no other : surviving the violent death of
someone you love / Kathleen O'Hara.
p. cm.
1. Bereavement—Psychological aspects. 2. Grief.
3. Violent deaths—Psychological aspects. I. Title.
BF575.G7O29 2006
155.9'37—dc22
2006002289

ISBN: 1-56924-297-6
ISBN-13: 978-1-56924-297-1

9 8 7 6 5 4 3 2 1

Designed by India Amos, Neuwirth & Associates, Inc.
Printed in the United States of America

Author's Note

IN ORDER TO protect the privacy of individuals and families, I have changed the names of the people in the stories you will read—although in some cases, where the person agreed, I have used real names.

Some of the stories are composites of different experiences, which when combined, present powerful examples of what happens when violence strikes.

FOR AARON

I gave you to the world and it took you
I give you again and you will live

CONTENTS

FOREWORD

by Dan Gottlieb, PhD,
host of NPR's *Voices in the Family*

A GRIEF LIKE NO *Other* begins when Kathleen O'Hara picked up the telephone to find out that Aaron, the son she had recently sent to college, was missing. When I first heard Kathleen's story, I could only begin to imagine her frantic worry, the passionate wishes and prayers, and the inevitable nightmares that raced through her mind. I could try to imagine her terror because, as a parent, I have experienced fear bordering on terror when my children were not where they should be. But when I heard about the next call—the one that confirmed her worst nightmare that Aaron was murdered—I was no longer able to imagine her reaction.

Almost all of us will experience trauma at some point in our lives. Sometimes trauma begins with a doctor saying, "We have to talk," or a spouse telling us they want a divorce. Whatever form it takes, all trauma causes suffering. Some trauma we can identify with. Some trauma is unimaginable. All trauma isolates and alienates, but when no one dare imagine what you are experiencing, you are exquisitely alone with your pain.

That's why I was so surprised to hear Kathleen O'Hara was

willing and able to talk about her tragedy on the radio. Four years ago I invited her to be a guest on my *Voices in the Family* radio show aired on WHYY in Philadelphia. When I went down the elevator to meet her in the lobby of the studio, I expected to see a woman in acute grief—pale complexion, rounded shoulders, and poor eye contact. I was prepared to be gentle and caring even though I was afraid to imagine what she was feeling.

Yet despite everything I imagined, I was greeted by a woman with clear eyes and a warm engaging smile that seemed to say, "It's okay, we can talk about this." In that moment, I realized that I was the one afraid to make eye contact. I felt both ashamed of my temerity and care for this amazing woman. All in one smile. Immediately, I wanted to get to know her better, to understand how she could survive this nightmare. I wanted to know where this agony lives in her head and heart and how she is able to function. I wanted to know all these things only partly because I thought it would be a painful but important radio show. On a deeper level, I wanted to know these things because I felt Kathleen O'Hara could add to my understanding of what it means to be human.

I was right. The show was powerful, as she told her horrible story in a way that was open, honest, and painful. In the years that followed, I have discovered I was also right about what she has to teach. I have come to know Kathleen as neither hero nor victim—just a woman who has endured tragedy and has been able to use the tools of her counseling training and her own spiritual background to cast a clear eye on the nature of trauma and recovery.

Research tells us that many people recover from trauma, depending on its severity. Those who make meaning out of their suffering are more likely to be resilient. The book you hold in your hand clearly represents Kathleen's insightful effort to make meaning out of her suffering. But because of her training, wisdom, and clear thinking, this book helps us understand the human response to tragedy.

Using her own story as background, Kathleen guides us through seven clear steps that begin with telling the story and slowly guide us through finding resources, facing pain, generating creativity, and discovering the "New World"—the place where survivors will find themselves after experiencing the seven stages found here. For those left behind in the wake of violence, the New World is a necessary destination—a place that allows survivors to live with the trauma and celebrate life in the face of extraordinary pain.

This nightmare broke Kathleen's heart. It broke her heart wide open. In reading this book, you will learn how trauma opens your heart. Following Kathleen's insightful guidance, you will also learn about the courage it takes to keep it opened.

ACKNOWLEDGMENTS

THERE ARE SO many people who helped in the genesis of this book. First, I want to thank those of you who told me your stories, and compelled me to reach inside my own personal and professional experience and find ways of making sense of it all and helping us endure this grief like no other.

I did not make this journey alone, and could not have. It has been this collective grief that has revealed a way to travel. I am grateful to everyone for sharing these most personal experiences generously and openly.

The idea for this book came out of our communal grief. Rachel Simon, a friend and mentor, helped me see that the book indeed could have a life and breath of its own and encouraged me to "write the book."

John Timpane's keen editorial skills helped to bring the idea out of the dark and into an early form and structure. His sense of humor made me laugh—at myself, and made the whole process so much more bearable!

Dan Gottlieb, my wise and wonderful friend, believed in me and the book and was kind enough to introduce me to Ed Claflin, who became my agent. Ed told me I did indeed have a book, and gave me hope that "my baby" would be born in the world.

He found Renée Sedliar, my editor at Marlowe & Company—and she became my midwife, teacher, and friend and helped me birth this book. She and I have shared laughter, grief, hope, and the belief that this book will help those who have lost someone they love to violence.

Renée, along with copy editor Iris Bass, showed me how to craft the book and stay true to its vision. I am deeply grateful to them and everyone who helped make something good come out of such a terrible experience.

I also want to thank Eric Schlosser, from whom I borrowed the title, from his article of the same name.

I thank my two children, Anna and Michael, for their love and support and examples of how to live life—no matter what. They are my greatest joy.

And to all of Aaron's friends, from Franciscan University, those in California and Colorado, and many other parts of the world: Thank you for being here with me—it is your spirit that reminds me of Aaron and how much he continues to be loved.

Aaron's Story

D O Y O U K N O W where your son is?"
It was a police detective calling from Steubenville, Ohio.
I clenched the phone, tried to speak. Finally, I heard my voice saying that I had just spoken to Aaron the previous day. When I had talked to him, I told the detective, Aaron was in Steubenville, safe in the house he was renting for the summer with two friends and classmates.

The officer already knew a few details—Aaron's address, the fact that he had just finished his sophomore year at Franciscan University, and, obviously, my telephone number. When it came my turn to ask some questions, the detective's replies were brief. Aaron was missing. Missing? How could he be *missing*?

I put down the phone. I felt tears running down my face; I couldn't speak; everything was moving and changing. Terror gripped me. My world had changed. It felt as if my life was shattering into a thousand pieces. As I was to learn, this is the nature of violence: Often, it is unexpected, unpredictable, chaotic, and above all, horrifying. It can strike at any time, any place. And, of course, it can happen to anyone.

It could be the death of someone we love or a friend or colleague. It can be a violent act of murder, robbery, rape, suicide, drug overdose, hate crime, domestic violence, terrorist attack, or vehicular homicide. Violence causes not only that person's death, but a catastrophic loss in our own lives. The world we once knew changes in a matter of moments into a new place: shocking, terrifying, uncharted. For me, it began with that phone call. This was the first step on a journey I did not want to take but, like all of us who are left behind in the wake of violence, I was forced to set out in a small boat in a turbulent ocean I had never even known existed.

The day was Monday, Memorial Day 1999. People were getting ready for barbecues. On streets all over America, there were parades for fallen heroes. We gathered in my living room: my friend Robert; my daughter Anna, then eighteen; and my youngest son Michael, who was fourteen. Years before, I had been divorced from my children's father, Howard. Howard and I had remained close even after the divorce, but in 1992 he had died suddenly from a heart attack, a loss that profoundly affected my children and me.

Now we were being plunged into another world of trauma. A new story had begun—a story of unutterable grief, transformation, death, and life. It was a story I would tell many times in the coming years. In fact, this very experience of telling my story would become the foundation for the first stage in the Seven-Stage Journey you will find in this book.

 Stage 1: The Journey Begins—Telling Your Story. Our stories are the container for all the events, emotions, details, and consequences of what happened when we lose a loved one to violence. Our stories tell about a special kind of grief, one we can never be prepared for. The element of violence makes our stories that much more difficult to tell and presents many challenges we must learn to live with. Speaking out helps us gain mastery over our emotions and eventually provides us with a way of measuring how far we have come in our journey, how well we are handling the enormous changes we have encountered.

Outside, the sun glared. In the shaded living room, Robert, Anna, Michael, and I sat together, trying to make sense of what little we knew: Aaron and his housemate Brian were both missing. Andrew, the third student in their rental, was now with the police. Perhaps even as we sat there, wondering, he was telling the police that all was well. But if so, wouldn't they call us at once? It was gut-wrenching to be in the dark. When would we know what was going on?

I'd talked to Aaron the day before. It was a normal conversation, like the ones we always had. "Hi, mom," he had said. "I got an A in statistics!" I'd laughed, knowing that although Aaron was very intelligent, he didn't always apply himself to academics, "That's great, son—I wish you had come home for Memorial Day." He'd then promised me he would come home as soon as the summer session was over. As I tried to make sense of what the detective had told me, I found myself going over and over in my head, that last conversation with Aaron. There had been nothing unusual about it at all. He'd said that he was going to go to Mass and would be meeting up with Brian later on. I remember saying, "Okay, son, I'll see you soon, love you," and hanging up the phone. Was there something I had missed in that conversation? Something he wasn't telling me? No, I knew there wasn't—I knew my son.

Now, sitting in my living room, I questioned his siblings to get more information, but there was precious little that any of us knew. Where were Aaron and Brian's friends? What did they know about his disappearance? How could I get in touch with them, as most of them had gone home for the summer? Franciscan University, a small, tightly knit community of faculty and young people, is a Catholic college. The kids that go there want to live "the life," as they call it. What they mean by that—what drew Aaron there—is a commitment to helping others. Faith is a crucial part of that community. So is the fellowship and close interrelationship of people committed to a common faith and principles. Aaron belonged to a close network of friends there.

Finally, late in the afternoon, the calls started coming in. Now the network was buzzing. Everyone was trying to figure out what had happened to Brian and my son. As the phone calls continued and became more prolonged, we began to piece together a chronology. Aaron's friends had seen him 6:00 p.m. at Mass the evening before. We learned that Brian had driven from his home in Columbus, Ohio, in his mother's black Chevy Blazer, meeting up with Aaron sometime in the evening.

As the day drew to a close, I began making calls to the police. Detective John Lelliss was in charge of the case. It was he who had called to ask where Aaron was. Now he let me know what the police had learned from Aaron and Brian's housemate.

Andrew had stayed up late the previous night, sitting on the porch, talking to a friend. Sometime after midnight, he went to his room. As he passed through the living room and headed upstairs, he saw Brian asleep on the couch. Andrew noticed that the door to Aaron's room was closed, and assumed that he was asleep. He didn't know, however, whether Aaron was actually in the room.

Lelliss now told me that the police had found blood on the wall and bed of Aaron's room.

"How much blood?" I wanted to know. My detached voice did not match what I was feeling. I told myself, maybe it's not Aaron's blood, maybe he wasn't there. After all, Andrew only *thought* Aaron had been in his room.

Lelliss had no way of knowing at that time how much blood there was or whether the blood was Aaron's. The investigation would continue. That was all he could tell me.

With every detail, my shock increased. I was shutting down. Terror was forcing my old life out of me, and I felt like I was suspended in the middle, between the world I had known and a shattered, out-of-control universe. I was trying to hold on to anything I could. I watched the rational, reasonable side of me answer questions, make assumptions, calculate options, but my emotional self was swirling down a drain into a dark hole.

Already, I wondered whether I would be able to survive this. Was it something I could endure or would it destroy me? Would my inner resources serve me as they had in the past or would they just not work? And the worst question of all: if Aaron was gone, could I live?

 Stage 2: Life Preservers—Discovering the Eight Qualities. Having talked to many people who have endured violent trauma, I have found that this is the way we get through it. In the beginning, we go into shock, which protects us from the terrible event. We split off into compartments so we can cope. One compartment might be trying to figure out what's going on; another might be trying to control emotions; yet another is surely entering the hellish world of fear and terror. Finally, as the shock wears off, we have to locate and gather whatever strength and inner resources we have in order to go on. These inner resources can be described as the eight qualities of courage, hope, faith/ spirituality, optimism, humor, patience, joy, and compassion— qualities that I would have to discover and learn how to use.

At that time, my immediate inner resources were prayer and meditation, faith, courage, hope, fortitude, and an unshakable belief that no matter what happens, life goes on.

We suffer because we are human, I told myself. We hope for the grace to shoulder our burdens. We face what life gives to us, whether it is unfair or not. We struggle to go on, when everything inside screams that we cannot. I know all that, I could say to myself. But would that be enough? Surely, this would be my greatest test.

The Franciscan network yielded bits and pieces of information, mostly about Aaron and Brian's whereabouts the night before. Still, I couldn't get the information I desperately wanted. The police knew more than they were telling me—I was certain of that. Why wouldn't they tell me everything?

At the same time, my denial was insistent. I told myself that Aaron would call any minute to explain the mixup. He had gotten up early and gone to a friend's house. Any moment, he would call to say, "Mom, geez, I only went out to visit a friend. Why all the drama?" I could almost convince myself this would happen shortly and there was nothing to worry about.

 Stage 3: Lighthouses in the Harbor—Finding Guidance and Resources. When a violent trauma occurs, we need people to support and guide us through the tremendous struggles we will encounter in our journey through grief and loss. We cannot do it alone. We need to find outer resources which, like lighthouses in the harbor, will help us find our way. At first, these outer resources will come from the immediate group of people surrounding the event.

During this period of uncertainty, my children and I stuck close to one another and tried to support each other as much as we were able. I had the strong support of my family, close and extended, and the wonderful friends I had made through the years, especially my friend Judy, who lived nearby.

In addition, many people came to Franciscan from all over the country to be with us and offer whatever they could to support us. Rachel Muha, Brian's mother, and her family arrived in Steubenville and were remarkable people of faith and strength.

Franciscan University conducted three prayer services a day. I met many of Aaron's college friends, who were to become close friends of mine through the years. I was surrounded by many, many people who held vigil with us. They searched, prayed, and struggled; we became united in one effort.

EARLY TUESDAY MORNING, Robert came to pick up Anna, Michael, and me. He was driving us to Steubenville; we were going to look for Aaron. As we drove up the Pennsylvania Turnpike, I looked out on the beauty of the rolling green hills. I found it hard to reconcile this tranquil scene with what I was about to face.

Detective Lelliss was a tall, earnest man who tried his best to help us understand what was going on. He told me that the house

Aaron, Brian, and Andrew shared had been broken into early the previous morning. Andrew had woken up, hearing a commotion downstairs. He'd known something was wrong. Jumping out his bedroom window, he had dropped to the ground outside, calling for Aaron and Brian. Peering in the living-room window, he had seen a man with a white handkerchief around his face. Upon hearing Andrew, the man had whirled around.

"Oh, fuck, there's another one!" Andrew had heard the man yell.

Andrew had raced to the nearest neighbor he knew, to call the police. By the time he'd returned, the house was empty. Brian's Chevy Blazer was gone.

Later, the police had spotted two men driving the Blazer in downtown Steubenville. When officers stopped the car, two men fled. One got away. The young man the police apprehended called himself Michael Poole. His real name was Terrell Yarbrough.

The Blazer was being searched. There was blood in the car.

Detective Lelliss held up a plastic bag. In the bright fluorescent light, against the background of yellow walls, I saw a blue plastic rosary, its crucifix broken. "Do you recognize this?"

I felt sick. Why was he showing me the rosary? Why was the cross broken? It was the kind of rosary given out at any service. Was it Aaron's? I had no way of knowing. My son had one, but so did practically everyone on campus.

Back at our hotel, I felt as though the world was closing in on me. Fear and anxiety gripped me; I wasn't going to be able to do this. I wanted to run away and pretend nothing had happened. Waves of hysteria started to overwhelm me. I went into the bathroom and took a long, hot shower. I wanted to rinse all this off me. I was trying to get some kind of grip. What could I hold on to?

Afterward, I went out to the courtyard outside my room. It was a still, warm evening. There was a lovely big tree in the center of the courtyard. Suddenly, two tiny birds flew out of the tree around and around my head. They were chattering, singing, and weaving through the air. I stopped and listened to them, I felt it was a message from

Aaron and Brian. I watched as they flew high in the sky, singing. I looked up and saw the evening star at twilight. Is that where they were? I knew it would be all right, that they were all right, no matter where they were. I felt peace, which I hadn't felt since the awful phone call. I turned to go inside the room, calm and ready.

 Stage 4: The Ocean of Grief—Learning to Ride the Waves. This is what we experience as a result of our trauma—overwhelming grief that we will have to learn to manage or it will drown us. Often we experience our grief like waves of the ocean; powerful, intense, with little or no warning. We will have to learn how to ride them. The first year, we struggle with survival. We are still in shock for all that time. We are confronted by birthdays, anniversaries, holidays, all of which can trigger our grief, sometimes with even greater pain than its initial onset.

The investigation continued, yet there were still no signs of Aaron and Brian. On Wednesday, the police arrested Nathan "Boo" Herring, who had been with Terrell Yarborough the morning of the break-in. Thursday was another day of anguish and searching; we went from hotel to police station to the university and back again.

Friday morning, I woke up knowing that this was the day we would find Aaron. During my morning prayer and mediation, I felt the search coming to a close. It was June 4, five days since I received the phone call about his disappearance.

I prayed for the strength to face what I knew was coming. That morning, I had one foot in the world I could see and one in the world beyond sight; it was a peculiar sensation of being present in my body while my spirit was somewhere else, searching for my son.

We were sitting by the pool at the hotel. Anna and Michael were in their pool chairs talking with the other kids, and my brother Joe was nearby, along with several others.

The phone rang. Someone handed it to me. By that time, I knew Detective Lelliss's voice well:

"We found Aaron, and he is deceased."

Aaron and Brian had been found under two white rose bushes in the Pennsylvania woods, not far from the Starlake amphitheater. The pool, the people near me, all started to fade away. I opened my mouth because something came out of me from someplace I didn't even know existed. I started wailing, "Aaron, Aaron, Aaron!"

The force of my own voice sent me whirling. I wanted him to hear me, wherever he was. I wanted my voice to reach the sky, pierce it, grab him, and bring him back. I wanted him to know I was here and couldn't bear it without him. I wanted God to hear me.

Someone was coming toward me, trying to hold me, comfort me. "No!" I wailed, "No!" I tore away from outstretched hands. I thought, "Leave me alone. I want my son. There is no comfort now. Let me feel this."

Pain ripped through my body. I fell against a wall. I rubbed my hand against rough concrete until it bled. I saw the faces whirl around me. People were dropping to their knees, grabbing their heads, sobbing.

On my knees, I cried. And then, suddenly, I stopped. It was done. What I had suspected and feared from that first phone call was true. Aaron was dead.

I don't remember what happened after that. My children and I were drained, in shock. What now? What happens now? I prayed for strength, and put one foot in front of the other and did what was next. There were Anna and Michael to think about, and all the people here; there were things to do.

 Stage 5: Out in the Deep—Practicing the Three Principles. In time, I would come to understand what it means to live with the wreckage of life after a violent crime. When we learn to ride the waves of grief, they take us out to the deep part of the ocean. We are left alone, feeling abandoned, our old world gone. We feel lost; the hard, cold reality hits us and we are simply treading water, with no new world in sight. When we find ourselves in the deep, we then enter a new phase of

the journey: we will have to find a way out. I would later learn how to practice the three principles of acceptance, forgiveness, and gratitude.

I don't remember the next two days very clearly. I knew only that Aaron was gone. I was borne up in the stream of events by what I can only describe as grace and support. I walked, talked, made decisions, yet was numb and frozen inside, unable to decipher the meaning of what had just happened. I moved through the world in a dreamlike state, unsure of everything.

At the chapel during the university's memorial service, I imagined Aaron there with his friends, just a short while ago. I remembered bringing him to church when he was a child and how once, during a particularly long service, he fell asleep and his blond head bobbed back and forth.

IT WAS A beautiful service, although I remember few of its details. I could barely stand up, and wanted to run out the door screaming. Above all, I wanted to wake up. There was something wrong here. This could not have happened.

But I didn't run out the door, and I knew that this indeed did happen and that this service was to bring us all together. It was a service not only for Aaron and Brian, but those of us who were left behind, shocked, battered, exhausted. Afterward, carrying flowers, we quietly made the pilgrimage to the big gray house on the corner of McDowell Avenue. When I saw it, my blood ran cold. It had darkness all around. As I stepped onto the porch, I noticed small flowers growing out of the cracks on the side of the steps. We put our flowers all around the porch. Here was where my son spent his last night, sleeping in his bed, thinking he was safe. This memorial for Aaron and Brian was a way for us to honor them and make something good come out of such horror. Yet even as I did this, I recalled how, earlier that month, I had planted flowers for Mother's Day in my own garden at home.

Stage 6: The Coral Reef—Generating Creativity. When we experience something horrible, our humanity helps us express our pain in something beautiful. Our greatest art and achievements often begin with a story of grief and sorrow, transformed into something we give each other to honor the ones we lost and our struggle to survive.

There are many things we can do to transform our pain to growth and good. We can bring beauty out of even the most terrible of events. This creativity can help lead us out of the deep into the new world.

During the prayer service, I met Aaron's fraternity brothers. They called their fraternity the Prodigal Sons (though they referred to themselves in less exalted form as "the Prods"). Having flown in from different parts of the country to help look for Aaron, many had stayed for the service.

As we said prayers for Aaron and Brian on the porch, each of these boys came to me and offered himself as my son. I thought of Aaron, and how he would have wanted that. I thought of how evil seeks to destroy the good in the world. But I also believe that good triumphs over evil, no matter what. While this would be a belief that would challenge me in years to come, on that day, in front of the house where Aaron was murdered, I held onto these beliefs for strength on the journey which lay ahead.

Before we left, many of Aaron's friends were gathered at the pool, trying to escape the sweltering heat. I looked at the water and wanted to jump in. I went into my room and found a brightly colored, tie-dyed T-shirt and put it on with a pair of shorts. I ran out of the room and jumped in the pool, surprising everyone.

One by one, the kids jumped in, too, and we laughed and played and renewed ourselves in the water. We were all smiling, saying Aaron was laughing, too, that he could see us from wherever he was and that this is what he would have wanted us to do. We let the water take the pain and sorrow, and, for a moment, felt it all wash away.

Afterward, we said our final good-byes. As we drove out of the town where Aaron had spent his last days, we passed the police station, the campus, and the streets we had searched. We had come here to find Aaron and Brian, and we had. The search was over, but yet it was just beginning. Where and how would we find Aaron and Brian in our lives?

There was a traffic jam out on Route 22. I looked at the woods on the right-hand side of the road. Was this where Aaron had spent his last moments? Was *this* the place, or was it *there*? There was a shadow on the road ahead. We drove in silence. We were going back to Philadelphia to wait for Aaron's body to come home.

 Stage 7: Embracing the New World—Emerging Possibilities. All of us who experience the violent death of someone we love are plunged into a world we never wanted, a world we start out hating but somehow must make peace with. It is not an easy task. In fact, it seems impossible. The road is too hard, the cup too bitter. But it must be done. Life goes on and we are part of it, with our sorrow and hopefully, our joy. It would take me a long time to find the new world—a place I could live in.

When I left Steubenville, I had no idea of what I was about to encounter. I was still in shock. I was moving into a world I didn't want. In this world Aaron would no longer be with me. I would have to learn to live with that and the memory of the awful things that had happened to him.

But over the years I have learned what I needed to know—how to cross the ocean and embrace the new world of life for the survivors of a violent death. This new world is a piecing together of the one that was taken away, the one I was forced to enter, and the one I live in now, as I write this book for anyone who is a survivor of someone who has died as a result of violence.

I've listed the stages that I discovered throughout my own journey. I hope they will help you as they have helped me and the other survivors I have counseled in my own practice, as well as people I have met through victims' support organizations and other local and national groups. I have found that following the stages in order helps people to navigate this painful journey. While we won't ever forget the pain our loved ones suffered, we will learn how to continue living.

You can choose to begin reading at stage 1 and read through; you can also choose to start at any stage you wish. Ultimately, I'd like you to think of this book as one of your lighthouses in the harbor, a light to guide you through the dark times you will face. Whatever stage you are in right now, I hope this book will help you, in some way, to find a promising new world of your own.

A Grief Like No Other

The Journey Begins

TELLING YOUR STORY

Those who do not have power over the story that dominates their lives—the power to retell it, rethink it, deconstruct it, joke about it and change it as times change—truly are powerless, because they cannot think new thoughts.

—SALMAN RUSHDIE

OVERCOMING THE VIOLENT death of someone you love is the most harrowing journey of them all. Your grief is a grief like no other, and one which you would have done anything to avoid. But here you are—you must make this journey or perish. When violence strikes, your familiar, safe shores vanish, throwing you into a vast ocean of grief and loss. In that ocean, you will be tossed and battered and nearly destroyed. You will encounter the storms of anger, isolation, fear, and pain; try to find comfort and hope wherever you can; and suffer alone when you cannot.

Every journey starts with a story: how it began, what happened, and where you are now. Your story is powerful, overwhelming; you will need to overcome it, manage it, and gain power over its raw emotions. And you will need to shape it into something you can carry so that its weight doesn't crush you; something you will bring with you across that ocean into a new world.

Learning how to tell your story is the beginning of your seven-stage journey. It marks your departure from the everyday world you once knew. While the event will be different for each reader of this book, what you all have in common is that there is always a story, yours alone to tell, from your unique point of view. Not only do you have a very personal relationship to the events that happened, but the very nature of violent crime means that you must be prepared to tell your story over and over again, and to a variety of different audiences.

The story of how your loved died is one that will stay with you forever. It may dominate your life for a long time, maybe for the rest of your life. You cannot nor should you attempt to ignore it. You will need to be able to tell, retell, and rethink it many times through the years. It will reconstruct and change as times change, and hopefully it will contain humor and good things, too. Although you may not be able to believe this now, the pain within the story will become bearable; it will shrink to allow other feelings to emerge. As Rushdie tells us, if you do not gain power over it, you will not be able to think beyond that pain—you will become mired in your despair rather than helping yourself to move forward.

This chapter will give you guidelines and examples of how I and others who have experienced the violent death of someone we loved have shaped our powerful stories into a form we could manage. Here, I will also suggest ways you can tailor your story for different people and circumstances. It is important to have different versions for different purposes, such as to protect yourself from the insensitive and intrusive comments of other people, or to deal with professionals, such as doctors, for whom facts are of the essence.

How Our Grief Is Different

A VIOLENT DEATH forces whoever survives it into a nightmarish chain of events. You may hear the news, or actually discover the body, witness the event, or be part of the act itself. You are surrounded by medical or emergency personnel, police, detectives, coroners, media, and the legal system. Dealing with all these kinds of people and situations is never easy.

Chaos, shock, confusion, terror, anger, and explosive emotions may overwhelm you. Intrusive questions will have to be answered and insensitive people dealt with. You may be hounded by the media or accused by the police. You may have survived the actual violence and be plagued by guilt that you could do nothing to change what happened.

If the crime occurred at your home or the home of your loved one, you will have to deal with living in a crime scene and/or being an active part of an ongoing investigation.

The body of your loved one is taken away by strangers, or perhaps there is no body at all, only the vast, aching knowledge that the one you love cannot be found. Perhaps there has been a break-in, kidnapping, murder, rape, accident, attack, suicide, or a drug overdose. Or maybe you don't know what happened at all, and feel absolutely helpless to do anything.

You may have been the one who discovered the body, or you may have to go the morgue and identify it. Perhaps there will never be the discovery of a body or, like myself, you won't see the body when it is found.

Ultimately, you will have to make decisions you never thought you would have to make, tell people what happened when you haven't even begun to grasp it; often you will feel like you are the one taking care that they are not overburdened, while you find yourself strained beyond your human capacity.

In some cases you will stay up for days while you wait for answers that do not readily come. You will try to cope and hold your life together

continued

while, surely, you feel yourself slipping away into this nightmare—which is your reality now.

Our grief is a grief like no other. There is no warning, no time to say good-bye, no time to put things in order or tell the person whom you love the things you would want to. You will have none of these comforts, and instead be plunged into a world of terror and grief. You will have to face each of these challenges as they come.

It is possible that some of the most painful experiences you will need to face will be hearing what happened in the voices of others: police reports, medical statements, journalists' descriptions or discussions of the tragedy, or testimony heard during legal proceedings that may involve graphic detail of how your loved one died. Indeed, even if no actual crime was committed, the necessity of an ongoing relationship with the legal system will be but one of many ways in which your grief is different. The ramifications of such procedures are explored more fully in chapter 5; the appendix also provides resources for you to find victims advocacy groups and other organizations that can help you.

Speaking through the Pain:
Your Oral Story

IN THE BEGINNING, YOU WILL NEED HELP

One of your most immediate difficulties in the aftermath of a violent death is that you have to discuss the situation again and again, whether you want to or not. The police and/or medical personnel may require that you repeat the events in detail and, of course, you will have to inform your families, friends, and others who may need to know what has happened. While you may have already experienced the period of initial trauma, it is important here to review the beginning stages by recalling what happened.

From the moment you hear of your loved one's death, from the moment you learn of the violent act, you are forced to become a player in an unexpected scenario, one for which you have no script. Everything is happening very quickly; you are shocked by what you are seeing or hearing. You are not merely a spectator; you are living this. Almost immediately, you will need to inform other people of the events at hand. They will probably include members of your family, friends, relatives, doctors, nurses, and legal or other professionals involved with the situation.

You will need to be able to convey at least the rudimentary details of what happened and what you know so far, so that you can communicate to each person what he or she needs to know. You will need to fine-tune your story to solve problems, make necessary contacts, and engage the resources you need. This is often an overwhelming experience, as Richard, discovered:

> I came home one day to find my wife lying on the kitchen floor, unconscious. I didn't know what happened. I went into shock when I saw her lying there. I picked up the phone and called 911. The ambulance and police came immediately. They wanted to know what had happened. I didn't know anything except that I found her.

It occurred to me that the police were questioning me as though I knew something else, which I didn't. It was an awful experience. When we got to the hospital, the doctors tried to save Susan, but they couldn't. I was trying to figure out what happened and trying to tell the police and doctors and our families what I knew. I was asked so many questions and had to tell people what happened, but, the truth was, I didn't know.

Experiences like Richard's are overwhelming because, as the trauma unfolds, you don't fully know what is going on. However attentive you may even think you are, you are confused, struggling to understand what is happening, while a part of you is going into shock to protect yourself from terror and fear. During this time, the story is taking over your life as if a tidal wave. You cannot possibly gain power over it because it is enormous and unexpected at the moment it first hits you. You need other people to help you, so that you are not totally overwhelmed by it. As you collect and process the details of what has happened, you will want to have people close to you who can share that information and help piece the story together. This forms the basis of your story.

When your story begins, you will want to have people help you tell it. Richard asked his brother, Jason, to tell people what happened and gather new details. Jason helped by taking care of many things that had to be done, creating a buffer between Richard and the overwhelming demands of the situation.

CREATING YOUR SUPPORT TEAM

It is important to ask someone whom you trust to tell the story or otherwise act as your surrogate when you are just too tired or need a break. Protect yourself during the unfolding of the trauma. You will need your strength for many other important things.

Often, during trauma, people don't realize how much help they need and don't always know what or whom to ask for. It is important to keep in mind that you can and should ask for help at any time, for anything you need, drawing upon friends and relatives or even professionals for assistance, whether it is someone to tell others what happened, make phone calls, or even help you to remember to eat. People often say in such a circumstance, "What can I do?" or "Please call me if you need anything." Take them at their word, and give them a specific assignment or let them choose to do one, then step back and let them do it for you.

 IF YOU ARE a friend or relative of someone who is experiencing this kind of trauma, please come forward and offer what help you can. Remember, no one is thinking clearly at this time and everyone is trying to find their way, so if you can offer any kind of assistance, do it. Please see page 55 for ways you could make yourself useful.

SPEAKING THE UNSPEAKABLE

After the event, you are left with the raw power of your story. You will need to shape it into something you can carry so that its emotions do not drown you. This is not an easy thing to do. You may not want to discuss what has occurred, even to articulate it to yourself, because it is just too painful. It may make the trauma too immediate. However, as a therapist, I have seen the effects of *not* telling the story.

Keisha, a woman I met several years ago, was raped and her fiancé, Robert, murdered. She did not want to talk about what happened. At first, she was in denial—she simply wanted to get on with her life, and so underestimated the impact of the violence. But keeping the story inside was causing severe problems. She developed depression and anxiety; she tried to work and could not. It affected everything she did—and why wouldn't it? Surely, experiencing these violent acts was unspeakable and life shattering.

Her story was so painful that she did not even want to meet new people; it was easier for her to stay alone than to tell someone new something so terrible about her life. In her mistaken attitude of invulnerability, she actually had locked herself in with the experience, preventing her from ever moving beyond it. Ultimately, this caused so many problems, Keisha realized she had to talk about it; it was just too much to carry alone.

Not telling your story is like carrying a weight so heavy it crushes you. Carrying this burden takes all of your energy; keeping the story to yourself prevents you from getting the help or relief you need. You become isolated and afraid to meet new people because they might ask you questions. Preventing any disclosure of the secret restricts more and more of who you are or could be as a whole person. Worst of all, the story comes out in unexpected ways, such as in anger, and in reckless behaviors, such as drug and alcohol abuse.

While I was attending a town meeting in Philadelphia on youth violence, I heard a teacher share the following:

> One of my students, a fifteen-year-old girl named Kimberly, would pace the halls instead of coming into class. I would ask her to come in, but she would just walk up and down the halls. I wondered what was going on with her. Was she just another "discipline problem"?
>
> I finally asked her. After a while, she told me her parents had been murdered. She could not sit down; she walked, trying to figure out what to do. I was shocked, because even though these stories of violence are not new to our school, no one here knew about Kimberley. How could we help her if we didn't know what had happened to her?

Kimberly would have continued roaming the halls trying to figure out for herself what to do, had one person not cared enough to ask her why. But when she told the teacher what happened, she could begin to get help. Even though Kimberly did not have extended family to care for her and the school she attended was already overburdened with cases like hers, she did get counseling at school as the result of her disclosure. As a result, Kimberly learned the benefits of opening up and sharing her story: now, she was not alone.

As for Keisha, after her rape, this young woman told herself she wasn't going to share her story with anyone. However, she recognized that this wasn't going to work. Anxiety, depression, and anger were taking over her life. She realized she had to talk about it and, gradually, she was able to share her ordeal with others. When she started dating again and eventually met the man who would become her new fiancé, she knew that she had to tell him what had happened to her. Now, she was able to so, because she had worked on her resistance to telling her story, eventually gaining power over it.

Maya Angelou says, "There is no agony like bearing an untold story inside of you." While our stories are painful to tell, it is ultimately more painful to keep the story locked up inside.

SHAME AND STIGMA

You may feel shame about what happened and this may keep you from telling your story. You hold it inside because you feel it is too awful to tell. You may be afraid to tell people what happened because of their possible reactions regarding the victim, or for fear of what they might think of you. Many in this situation experience the stigma that surrounds violence. It is vital to your recovery that you find the courage to face and work through this.

Silence is deadly; it leaves you feeling hopeless, angry, and isolated. Talking about what happened is an important step in removing the stigma, by stopping the denial our culture perpetrates. Survivors often feel as if they are the ones with the problem, as though they are rejected by the very society they thought they were part of. You may feel as if you did something wrong, and unfortunately there may be people who sometimes unconsciously or unintentionally reinforce this notion. For example, when Aaron and Brian first disappeared, people whom I knew suggested that my son was involved in something I didn't know about, which must have been the reason he was missing.

I was hurt and shocked by these assumptions, then I realized that people need justification for violent crime, as if to say the only reason these things happen is because the victim somehow brought it upon himself. There seems to be a need to believe that violence can be controlled simply by staying "out of trouble."

The other, equally insensitive depiction of victims is the well-known fascination with murderers, especially serial killers. Their glamorization by Hollywood makes the lives of the victims inconsequential. The killer is the center of attention while the victim is forgotten, or made to seem weak or unable to outsmart his "opponent." I was shocked to visit a Web site which auctioned serial-killer memorabilia. It had things like locks of hair from Charles Manson, paintings and posters of other such criminals, and other information about recent extreme acts of violence. When I saw this Web site, I hung my head in shame, not for me but for a culture that takes so perverse a pleasure in the details about the murders and the murderers of our loved ones.

Those of us who are survivors discover that, beyond taking a lurid interest in the details of a violent crime, people may not want to hear about it; they don't want to know more about who the victim was, about your relationship with him or her. Please understand that this may be a defense mechanism; they may not mean to be cruel. They need to feel that this terrible tragedy is an anomaly, something distant from their everyday experiences, something that can't affect them. Violence blights the landscape of the perfect life, one in which people believe that these sorts of things do not happen in their neighborhood or to their loved ones. Perhaps this dissociation makes them feel safer.

However, if you have lost a loved one through suicide or a drug-related death, you may already know that people may indeed be unconsciously cruel and insensitive. They will make assumptions about your loved one that diminish the whole of that person's life. Regardless of how he or she died, you deserve to tell the whole story, without shame, without stigma. Coming out of the silence and spreading the whole, larger truth helps all of us face down the denial and ideas our culture perpetrates about violence and "good" or "bad" victims.

At the same town meeting where I heard Kimberly's story, I met Victoria Greene, a social worker who works in the prison system in Pennsylvania. She had the courage to stand up and tell the story of her only son, Emir's, murder. Victoria talked about how she was a single parent, did the right things for her children, brought them to church, and taught them right from wrong. She thought she was "enough" to keep her son out of the neighborhood gangs.

Emir was murdered in a drug-related homicide. Victoria has had to face people saying, "Well, what did you expect?" She has been excluded from much of the sympathy others receive for their children. She has fought the stigma attached to a "good" victim versus a "bad" victim. When Victoria speaks out, she confronts head on the issue of shame and denial. She tells us that we have the right to tell our story, without shame. Ultimately, Victoria started an organization called Every Murder Is Real, because she wanted to stand up and tell all Emir's story—not just how he died, but who he was.

TAILORING DIFFERENT VERSIONS

For many, the story becomes the dominating force in their life. It can have an obsessive, almost compulsive quality, especially the first year.

You wake up and it's the first thing you think about; when you go to bed, if you can sleep, it is the last thing you think about. Many report dreaming about it and having nightmares, too. Your life becomes consumed by the violence and its repercussions. Everything not connected with the story seems unimportant. Yet, you will meet people who do not know what happened, and you will need to tell them, when necessary. At the same time, you will want to want to become less compulsive about telling the story unnecessarily, and more particular in the details that you do tell people.

Krista, whose daughter Katy was killed by a drunk driver, said,

> In the beginning, after Katy died, my world was pretty
> small. My friends, family, Katy's school; everyone knew.
> My story was all I talked about. I felt like everyone
> already knew and I was protected. But later that year,
> I started to meet people and I felt really vulnerable.
> What was I going to tell them? I felt anxiety meeting
> new people. I both wanted to talk about Katy, and at
> the same time, dreaded telling them what happened.

You will meet people for whom you will need to have different
versions of your story ready to tell. In situations where you don't
know the person, you will have to decide whether and to whom to
tell your story. I would caution you here to remember that people
may be shocked to hear what you have to say. It is important to gauge
whether it is appropriate to tell them. While not talking about your
story at all is a dangerous form of denial, you do have the right to
choose when and to whom you should tell your story.

For example, while I have mastered my story in many different
ways, I can forget its raw power; Aaron's murder is by its very nature
shocking, especially when time or familiarity does not permit a full
telling. I try to discern whether a person is ready to hear my story
and then try to prepare them by saying, "I am sorry to say, I lost my
son." Then I decide how much to say based on how appropriate the
setting and their relationship to me is.

It will become very useful to tailor one version of your story into
a short, easily delivered form and have it ready when you need to tell
it in unfamiliar or public situations. This can be done by choosing a
few sentences that give the necessary information without setting
off waves of undesired anguish in either you or your listener.

For example, when people ask about my son, and I find it necessary to tell them what happened but do want to involve them or me
in the whole story, I use the following version: "My son Aaron and
his roommate Brian were students at the Franciscan University in
Steubenville, Ohio. On Memorial Day of 1999, their off-campus
house was broken into by two young men. The robbery went wrong;

they took my son and his friend to the woods in Pennsylvania and shot them."

This is the essence of what happened. I tell it in an almost dispassionate way because I have told it so many times, in so many ways, since it happened. It is easier to speak about my son's death in this form because I have tailored it into something I can handle, yet while still providing the most basic information. This form of the story protects me. This format stylizes the event, gives it a shape, and creates an objective, strong boundary between me and the actual event. By perfecting this form and using it when I need to, I am able to protect myself from the overwhelming emotions I once felt when I spoke about the murder. The story gives me a safe distance from which to tell it. What was once a destructive force that nearly killed me is now something I am able to manage, which is the whole point of this exercise.

Tailoring the story also has the advantage of privacy. I do not have to share my grief and sorrow every time I share my story. I do not wish to have such intimacy with everyone, all the time. By tailoring your story, you will have a way to share the essentials without engaging in a degree of intimacy that you may not wish to have with that person.

Try this exercise: Construct three sentences about what happened, including the following:

+ The person's name
+ Your relationship to the person
+ When the person was killed
+ A brief description of what happened

The following shows how Krista tailored her story:

> My daughter, Katy, was three years old. In 2000, my husband and I were driving home from a visit to my parents. Our car was hit by a drunk driver and Katy did not survive.

As you can see, this version is tailored to give the minimum of facts to convey what happened. It gives Krista a strong but short story that she can master and use when she needs it. It also protects her from all the details, which may bring up too much emotion in public settings.

Remember that, in the beginning, the story of what happened will be all there is. It *will* consume your life. But as time goes on, especially after the first year, your story will become incorporated into your life; and, someday in the future, it will become something you have learned to carry so well, you will be able to look at it without the pain you feel initially, and many people you meet will not imagine that such a thing had ever happened to you. They and you, yourself, will know you as you really are, as your whole person, and not as the shell left over from one horrific experience.

I know this is hard to believe, especially if you are reading this in your first year, but you will have your own life back again. Carolyn founded a local support group after her daughter Donna was murdered. She said this about her experience:

> Now twenty-seven years later, it is like a bank of clouds on the horizon. Always there, but distant. Although on some days, the clouds turn more gray.

OWNING YOUR STORY

As I mentioned, there will be times when you don't want to tell what happened to your loved one, or it isn't appropriate, or you don't want to answer questions. What do you do? The answer is simple: you are within your rights not to answer any question you don't want to, or to not tell your story when you feel too vulnerable, or to refuse to discuss the matter with someone whose business you do not feel it is.

Many times, people ask me the question I dread: "How many

children do you have?" This question, innocent in itself, is very painful to me. It brings up the fact that I used to have three children and now I have two, and that the whole awful mess happened, and, furthermore, that I should even feel I have to explain it. I've changed my response over the years. I now simply say "Three." If I am asked for more detail and I feel like I want to answer, I will. Sometimes, though, I don't want to talk about the fact that Aaron is dead. I change the subject or stop the conversation.

You can stop these kinds of conversations at any time, if you feel they are too intimate and upsetting. If you do not want to answer specific questions about the person who died or how it happened, say so. It's perfectly fine to say to someone: "You know, I just can't say any more about it." People will understand, and if they don't you are within your rights to end the conversation as politely as you can.

When Richard talks about his wife, Susan, and people want to focus on the details he tells them, "You know, I don't want to focus on that, but I will tell you that Susan was a wonderful person, wife, and mother. That is what I want to tell you about."

You are entitled to tell your story differently to people when and how you choose. The way you tell it may not be the same as what is explained by other family members. For example, some relatives may want to leave the details of violence out. Others may want to include them because they feel their story cannot be told without them.

Each person will tell the story as he or she feel it happened to him/her, and as his/her level of comfort and understanding permits. Recognize that you and everyone else involved with the loss of your loved one is struggling with the raw power of emotions and details. This is not a contest to see how much more strongly one person expresses feelings, or can suppress them, or about which of you has the right to have loved the deceased more. Allow yourself to tell your story, and others, theirs, in the way that feels best for each of you.

THERE ARE GOOD THINGS, TOO

You may miss talking about your loved one and who he or she was. You miss hearing the person's name and relish a chance to say it. I remember, after the first year Aaron died, I really missed that, hearing and saying his name. It was a strange thing; he was in my thoughts and yet the occasions for using his name became fewer and fewer—people just didn't talk about him anymore; when they did, even when I did, everything about him was in the past, not the present.

I was asked to be the speaker at the anniversary dinner of Compassionate Friends, a support group for family members who have lost a child. The dinner happened to be scheduled the week before Memorial Day, five years after Aaron's death.

I was glad to have the opportunity to tell his story, because I told the audience not just the horror of what happened, but what Aaron was like. I had an opportunity to tell them about my son, and say his name, Aaron—and for that hour, he was alive.

There are good reasons for telling your story; when these occur, you can experience comfort, love, and even a bit of the miraculous, as did Maya, a woman I met at one of my retreats:

> We gathered at the funeral of my father, Daniel. He should never have gone to the store that night, but there was nothing I could do about it . . . it happened. I was so angry. What would I do now without my father? As we stood at the grave while the priest said prayers, I saw how many of us were there. All around were his family, my family, brothers, sisters, aunts, uncles, children, cousins, and friends. It was a sea of people and I looked up and there was a rainbow in the gray sky. It seemed to form an arc above all of us! I realized my father's love was there, over us all. He lived in every one of us and he would be there for me, in their smiles, their faces, their hearts.

Writing Your Story:
The Power of Pen and Paper

MANY OF US do not think of ourselves as storytellers or authors. Instead, we listen to others or read them in books. We watch movies or television about other people's lives. We stand on the sidelines, waiting for someone to tell us what our stories are, or listening to theirs.

The immediate, powerful momentum of our experience changes that. We are thrust into the center of the action. We are not watching, or living vicariously, but instead living a visceral, compelling experience.

We struggle with our story, trying to hold it, shape it, keep it from crushing us. Writing it down can help. It provides a practical vehicle to contain our feelings, experiences, and growth. It gives us some immediate objectivity and distance from the actual events and provides a record for the future of what happened.

SUPPORT

Your writing will bring up a variety of feelings. Make sure you have some kind of good support system for your work. I will be asking you to form a much more detailed support network in stage 3, which is about finding guidance and resources; but for now, have someone you can talk to when these feelings come up. This could be a trusted friend or family member, a therapist, or clergy.

TOOLS

You may decide to write on your computer, or to handwrite your story, using something as simple as a notebook or pad. Many people decide to purchase a beautiful journal, perhaps with a cover that reminds them of their loved one. Renata chose one with a lovely paisley cover that reminded her of Nancy, her cousin, who was killed. Whether you use a computer or a physical book, you may even wish to paste in mementos of the person, such as photographs or extracts from e-mails you had exchanged. Include whatever enables you to tell your story fully.

However you keep it, you may want to consider using the journal for doing the exercises presented in this book, as well as your personal writing. The choice is up to you. However, the advantage to using a daily journal is that it is both the story of what happened to your loved one, but also of your journey afterward.

PLACE

The place where you choose to write is up to you and dependent upon your circumstances. If you are able to find a quiet place, all the better, because you will have more privacy for your writing and your feelings. Stacey, whose childhood friend, Cara, was murdered coming home from a party, told me, "I decided I was going to try and write down what happened. My house is noisy and crowded, but we do have an attic. I went up there and it became my haven. I started writing among the trunks of old clothes and toys and things from my childhood. It turned out to be the best place for me."

For Krista, the place was at her kitchen table after everyone went to bed. There, while everyone was asleep, she wrote about Katy.

TIME

Finding and scheduling time is really about setting time aside so you can begin your work with the minimum of interruption. Writing your story will be an emotional task, so you will need to create a time when you can deal with your feelings.

For me, at first, there didn't seem to be a good time, so I just said, "Today, I am going to try and write something." It may be helpful to say you are going to write for one-half hour at such and such a time, and see what happens. If you do schedule that time and cannot write, do not worry; you can pick it up again when you feel stronger. Remember, you haven't been down this road before and you need to pay attention to how you feel and what is comfortable for you to accomplish—it's your journey and your story.

HOW TO START

Writing your story is a practical exercise of putting the words in a shape and form you can use in many different ways. When you sit down to write, you may find that your mind is full of random thoughts and images about the violence. You can choose to begin with any of these thoughts or images. Many people find it easier to start with their first knowledge of the event itself. Earlier in this book, I began the story of Aaron with that awful phone call from the detective in Steubenville. Wherever you start is fine, the point is to write something down.

If you can't think of a place to start, try to use the following suggestions:

+ Write, "This is the story of what happened; it all began on. . . ."
+ Name the date, place, and time.
+ Name the people involved and their relationship to you.
+ Write the first thing that happened (phone call, or other first inkling that something was wrong).
+ What happened then? (Try to write the main events, for example: we waited at my house for information, then we went Steubenville. . . .)
+ What was the outcome?

Do not be critical of yourself, of the style in which you are writing, or even of your spelling or grammar; you're very brave to attempt this. Don't slow down the flow to try to perfect what you are saying. If you need to stop, then stop. Pick it up later, when you feel you can. This exercise will be interwoven with your grief, and rightfully so. You may not be able to write for very long; that's fine. Remember to talk to someone afterward, if you need to.

THE WAY YOU WERE

It is important to remember who you were the day *before* the event happened. When you are faced with these violent events, you lose the connection with your immediate sense of self—your place in a world larger than the immediate circumstance. It's like being swept form the shore of your life against your will, and try as you might, you cannot swim back; during this strange interlude, what is most familiar to you may seem foreign, strange, even invisible. You need to remember your identity and the touchstones within your usual landscape because, as you move through this journey, you need to believe that someday, as you put the pieces back together, you will find your place again in the world, although not, perhaps, in the way you imagine.

When I met Claire, she and I worked on telling and writing her story. I asked her who she was the day before her husband, Jim, was murdered. She could barely remember her life untouched by violence but it was important for her to hold on a picture of who she was—not "had been," as a closed-off entity—and believe that, as time passed, she would become that person, to a great extent, again. She said,

> I was young then, even though it was less than a year ago . . . I thought that my world was perfect. The house, the garden, my husband and children. I worried about small things, like what to make for dinner or would the children's teeth need braces, and [about] saving money for their future educations. I worried whether I was good enough, or whether people liked me. But I was also dependable, stable, and generally optimistic. I remember thinking the world was a lovely place. When Jim was murdered, that all changed—the world became a horrible place.

It was not an easy task for Claire, but she persevered. She told me her story of before, during, and after the tragedy happened. By talking her way through her memories and feelings, she was able to find a place for herself again. When finally she did reconnect with the person she was *before* the murder, she wasn't the same as before, but she could at least recognize herself as someone she wanted to be. This did not happen overnight for Claire, but instead was a gradual process of learning to live again.

Use the following writing exercise to help you remember who you were the day the violence happened.

+ Date, time
+ Weather
+ I was happy, sad, depressed, optimistic . . .
+ I liked doing the following things . . .
+ I worked at . . .
+ My family members were . . .
+ People would describe me as . . .
+ I worried about . . .
+ I had dreams of becoming . . .

This writing exercise does not have to be long; it simply needs to be a few notes about who you were the day the trauma happened. A note about support: this exercise is something you can do with someone else, a friend or family member who knows you and can help you answer these questions.

Here's how I wrote mine:

> It was May 31, 1999, Memorial Day. It was hot and dry. I was planning to have a barbecue that day. I was the mother of three children. I was a therapist. I was generally optimistic, adventurous, courageous, caring, but also fearful, anxious, and impatient. I liked to take walks in nature, cook, travel, and start new projects. I had returned from Colorado the year before and was looking forward to working and living in Philadelphia and being with my children.

You can use my example to help you with this exercise; remember, it is simply to remind you of who you were before the violence.

WRITING AS HEALING

When I returned home to Philadelphia from Steubenville and the funeral was over, the house became quieter, there were fewer distractions, and I was left alone for the most part. My story consumed me. I couldn't think of anything else, because that's all there was in this new, terrible world I inhabited. Every moment seemed to relate in some way to Aaron's murder. I was overwhelmed. I couldn't imagine how anything like this could have occurred. I could not wrap my mind around it; it was just too big, too threatening. Nonetheless, I knew I had to start to gain some power over it or it would destroy me.

During the first few months, I told my story, yet most people I knew already knew the details. Their lives went on, while my world had shrunk into my immediate surroundings.

I attempted to write everything down, with varying degrees of success. In the beginning, every time I tried to write, I would stumble and agonize over every word. I cried so much, I had to stop and start, and, sometimes I couldn't write at all. I hated my story and wanted to rip it up when it was done. Several times I did destroy it and tried to ignore the whole thing, hoping I would somehow forget about it. I didn't.

I couldn't face the facts of what happened to my son. I was battered, shell-shocked, but I persevered because I knew it would help me, and it did. I wrote an article for *Catholic Faith and Family* magazine. It was called "Finding Light in the Darkness," and was about my struggle with acceptance. There was a picture of me and Aaron on his fourth birthday, with him blowing out the candles. Writing that article was healing but sorrowful. Yet, despite the sadness, it helped me to write about my son, and let people know what I was struggling with, so that it could help them. Later, I helped others write their stories. Many found it painful, difficult, but yet most people reported that it was a healing experience, one they were glad they did.

THE BENEFITS OF WRITING

At first, Richard found the thought of writing about Susan's death appalling, yet he eventually overcame his resistance to writing:

> When my wife was murdered, the last thing I wanted to do was talk about it, and even less did I want to write about it. I felt it was too horrible. How do you go into the "normal" world of business and tell people your wife was murdered and you don't know who did it?
>
> I found that people either reacted with horror or wanted to know the details of the crime. Their curiosity sometimes repelled me. Why they so fascinated with every detail, yet were not concerned about Susan? I tried to keep it all inside.
>
> The trouble was, I couldn't sleep. I stayed awake thinking about Susan and what happened; what would I do now and how would I help the kids? I would think of ways I could catch her murderer and what I would do to him when I did.
>
> During the day, I couldn't concentrate at business meetings, because my mind would shut down, or start thinking about what happened; I couldn't get control over my thoughts, it was hard to stay focused.
>
> Finally, I decided to do something about it and follow the advice I was given about writing it down. This was tough, but I did it. It helped. I put my feelings into the writing and I could see them on paper and handle them better.

The benefits to Richard were many. He found a form for his thoughts, a container for his feelings. It was something tangible he could see and begin to gain control over. The story wasn't dominating him as it had once had. Writing his story wasn't a magic formula, where everything was now under control, but rather a beginning.

Remember, one of the greatest benefits of telling and writing your story is to take control over it. By articulating your thoughts and feelings, you will be able to shape and contain it toward a version you can begin to tell, retell, and reshape it for the future.

When you have written down your story, take a moment and congratulate yourself. You have taken the first steps toward transforming this tremendous burden into something you can use and gain power over.

FORGOTTEN DETAILS

You may notice, as you read your story that, remarkably enough, you have forgotten some of the details. If this happens to you and you feel you need to add more details, then ask someone who knows them to supply them to you. You may want to start the conversation with someone who was there, or who had a different relationship with your loved one, by asking if they remember a certain detail. You can tell the person that he or she can be honest with you, that you really don't remember and need to have the information.

This will have the benefit of forcing you to share your story with others and obtain their perspectives. You may be surprised at what they tell you and how that diverges from what is in your memory; remarkable healing qualities may emerge from these conversations.

Deidre had lost her brother, Ben, when he tried to defend someone who was being robbed. She realized she had forgotten what the weather was like the day of the funeral, so she called her sister, Sara. During the conversation, Deidre and Sara shared not only what kind of a day it was but, when Sara discovered Deidre was writing about it, she began writing her own account. From this discussion, they were able to from an even deeper bond and decided later to write a family history for their children about Uncle Benjamin and what he was like. It became a beautiful memorial to their brother.

There is another reason for recalling or finding out the details: so that you will not be surprised or shocked again after the event. For example, when I went to the trials of the men accused of his murder, a year after Aaron's death, I wanted to know the details. Not because I wanted to hear about the horror; on the contrary, it was excruciating to sit through such brutal testimony. It nearly destroyed me. But I had to know what happened to my son. I also didn't want to hear these details later on, from strangers, piecemeal, and be shocked all over again. I was willing to hear it once and for all, instead of as vague rumors and surprises that would set me back for days. Some of those details I wrote about, and others just made me too sad to ever think about again. The point was, I heard as much as there was to hear; no one knew something *I* didn't, about my son.

IT'S YOURS NOW

Deciding the level of detail you want to hear and include will be up to you and what you feel you are able to manage. Once you have the details you want, and have included them in your writing, you can step back and look at what you have written. It's yours now; you have accomplished something you can use in many ways, whether as simply an account for you to put away, or something you can show people or turn into a creative project, especially when you reach stage 6.

Like Deidre and Sara, you may want to use this writing as the basis for an uplifting document in the future, surpassing its initial purpose as a personal record of tragedy. Relatives, perhaps a generation not yet born, may want to know about what happened. Your writing may become the foundation for a family memorial.

Lisa wanted to write about her mother who was killed by a drunk driver:

I wanted to tell the story of my mother, not just the terrible event that killed her, but who she was. I wanted people to understand how much she was loved; what she was like and how she grew up. I wrote a story about my mother and her life and it helped me to not only grieve for her, but to celebrate her life. This story was a wonderful gift to me, and to the rest of my family, just like she was. I know that long after I am gone, there will be a record of Marie, the first member of our family to be born here in America.

When you write your story, remember that the violence is only a part of it, although at first it will seem like all of it. But there are other parts: the goodness of human nature, how people reached out to you, and the occasional surprising miraculous things that happened. Write about them, too.

There are no rules for this kind of writing. You can do as little or as much as you wish. You can put it in any form you wish. This is your journey and only you can choose the way you make your voyage.

A GOOD AND BRAVE BEGINNING

In deciding to and how to tell your story, you have made a good and brave beginning.

Eventually, the story will become like the clouds on the horizon, sometimes distant, sometimes full of thunder and rain, and on some days, a soft white snow will fall.

For now, with your story in heart and hand, you can commend yourself on the hard work you have done and move on to the next stage, where you will discover how to use your life preservers—the eight qualities that will protect you as you cross the deep ocean that is grief.

Stage 2

Life Preservers

DISCOVERING THE EIGHT QUALITIES

THIS CHAPTER PRESENTS the eight qualities that are the life preservers you will use to keep you safe on your journey. They will help you stay afloat, keep you from drowning, and comfort you when you are alone. The eight qualities are characteristics you either already possess or need to develop. You will need every one of these qualities for when the waves of sorrow threaten to capsize you:

1. Courage
2. Hope
3. Faith/Spirituality
4. Optimism
5. Humor
6. Patience
7. Joy
8. Compassion

Just as the purpose of writing and telling of your story in stage I was to contain the tragedy into a shape and size you can carry and master, the purpose of this current stage is to help you to develop these eight necessary life preservers to help you bear the weight of your story and thus keep you afloat.

I have experienced and witnessed the destruction violence brings into our lives: despair, suicide, depression, hopelessness, and rage. In the aftermath of violence, many engage in behaviors they wouldn't otherwise: alcoholism, addictions, additional forms of violence, and ruined relationships are problems survivors may encounter during their grief. Lives may be destroyed, broken. Many don't make it to the other side of the ocean: the loss or its circumstances are just too devastating, the damage too deep.

This chapter presents the things you can do to prevent being sucked under the surface: qualities you must learn to recognize, appreciate, and apply.

What Life Expects of Us

MAN'S SEARCH FOR MEANING is Viktor Frankl's stark account of his imprisonment in concentration camps during World War II. He endured and observed unbelievable violence. He lost most of his family. After the camp was liberated, he went on to develop a form of therapy called Logotherapy.

In assessing his experience Frankl said,

> What was really needed was a fundamental change in our attitude toward life. We had to learn ourselves and, furthermore, we had to teach the despairing men, [in the camps] that *it did not really matter what we expected from life, but rather what life expected from us.* We needed to stop asking about the meaning of life, and instead to think of ourselves as those who were being questioned by life.

When extreme violence occurs to a loved one, we are being questioned by life: What does it expect of us?

Life expects us to step up and meet the challenges it has given us. It does not expect us to understand, nor does it give reasons for what happens. It does not pretend to be fair nor does it care what plans we had in mind. It is only for us to answer the question with another: Will we be able to meet life's challenges?

On the fourth anniversary of Aaron's death, I was asked to give a homily for a memorial mass for friends and families of those who lost children. I began by saying, "Each one of us belongs to a club we never, in our worst nightmare, wanted to belong to." This was true; not one of us in that church wanted to be there that evening. We all had had expectations that our children would grow up safe. No one, including me, thought our child would be buried before us.

Your loss will be different from mine, yet your task, the task that life has given you and expects you to master, is to carry your burden and live again. There is no magic formula to escape suffering. No one can suffer for you—you must do it yourself. But you do not have to suffer alone, or without resources. You have an opportunity to choose the way in which you will bear the burden life has given you. Will you meet it and allow it to transform you, or cower before it and permit it to further victimize you?

Using the Eight Qualities

THE PHILOSOPHER FRIEDRICH Nietzsche said, "Lord, make me worthy of my suffering." Surviving the violence done to a loved one is not an easy task—on the contrary, it will be the hardest thing you will ever do. Yet, it is the one thing that is asked of you. The eight qualities I have listed are not out of your reach—you have only to reach out to them for help, and they will be there to assist you on your journey.

Throughout the years, I have found that many of us have qualities we are not aware of. We may have thought we were strong or optimistic, maybe smart or personable, but often we do not give much thought about the "stuff" we are made of until the unthinkable happens. It is that trauma which will force us to face our inner selves and discover our true mettle.

Courage

COURAGE IS THE most important quality of the eight to have. Even if you don't think you have it, you must act as though you do! By that, I mean you need to believe you can make this journey, even if every part of you feels you cannot. Just the fact that you are reading this book shows you have the desire to survive, despite the terrible event you have experienced.

For some, the word *courage* conjures up an image of the hero or heroine doing battle with overwhelming forces. In fact, that is exactly what you are doing when you strive to overcome the violent death of someone you love. In the beginning, you may have the kind of courage that propels you into action, to save someone or yourself, or simply to keep from collapsing. You may go into shock and yet at the same time courage may enable you to do things you didn't know you were capable of, such as making decisions or staying up for days while you wait for news.

Later, you will need courage not only to survive, but to learn how to live again. This kind of courage has to do with the willingness to do what life demands of you. It is a sustained effort to continue, despite your feelings of despair, hopelessness, and grief.

Barbara had lost her husband, Steven, in the 9/11 attacks. She said the following about courage:

> How could I do this? How could I live again after Steven was killed? I wasn't a courageous person, in fact, I made it a point to avoid things rather than take a risk. It was Steve who kept everything safe for me, now he was gone and I had to learn to live in the world

without him. I found my courage because I had to—I
still had the children to think of—and I needed to find
the courage to live for them. I found a part of me that
I didn't know I had.

Barbara's story echoes what many survivors of violence have
had to do: find the courage to live for those who are still alive, and
that includes for yourself. Think of courage this way: it is the quality of commitment—a commitment to life, your life. There will
be many times when you may just want to give up because you're
hurting so much, or it's too hard. But rather than giving up, make
it your primary goal to gather the simple courage to face each day,
one day at a time.

The opposite of courage is fear, the specter that shadows every
step. Fear tells us we do not have courage, that we are weak and
powerless. Fear tells us that, because something bad did happen, it
will happen again. Fear is what keeps us stuck—living in a narrow,
mistrustful world where evil ever lurks just around the corner. Yes,
bad things happen, they truly do. However, we cannot allow our
fears to corrupt and limit everything we do. We must live as courageously as possible. This means living fully in the moment, despite
the absolute knowledge that life can change at any time.

A few years after Aaron died, I had a conversation about fear
with my grown children, Anna and Michael. We discussed how we
used to worry about things that never happened. But we couldn't
do that now, because something really bad *did* happen. It happened
once; it could happen again. We were struggling with the question of how we would live in a world where we now knew horrible
things occurred. The only answer for us was to try to have courage,
recognize our fears, and move through them. And when I chose
the tombstone for Aaron, I wanted a Celtic cross, with wild roses
around it, symbolizing our Celtic ancestry and the wild rose bush
under which he had been found. I chose the following inscription:
"Have courage, for I have overcome the world."

Think upon this quality, and see where you can bring it

meaningfully into your own life. Many times, courage will seem as far away as the shores of the world you left behind, but every day you can make a choice to be courageous. Try making a resolution in the morning to find the courage to face the day, or to find one courageous act to accomplish that day, such as to make a phone call you had been postponing, or to pack up and send to a charitable organization things that had belonged to your loved one.

You may want to find something to keep near you that symbolizes this quality. I kept a lovely calligraphy of the Chinese character for "courage" close to me at all times. It served as a reminder when I forgot, which was often. Your symbol can be as simple as a card with "courage" written on it and kept in your wallet, or printout of a poem you like. Try hanging it where you can see it, a picture of someone doing a courageous act. Read biographies of people who have handled great adversity with extraordinary courage. Think about relatives from past generations who had to cope with loss or upheaval, and remind yourself that you share their brave genes!

Remember, you do have courage already; the fact that you are still here is a testimony to it.

Hope

THIS QUALITY IS as important as courage. There is no doubt that, in this journey, you will be in the dark much of the time. Courage is the quality that gets you up in the morning and gives you the strength to face another day. But it is hope that gives you that small spark of light to hold on to when it's dark and the storms rage. Sometimes, you may not see or feel hope at all—your story is too heavy, your grief too strong. You truly believe the spark has blown out for good.

When Andrea's son Ryan committed suicide, she said,

> Where was hope? Ryan took his life; he had no hope and neither did I. Why should I? My despair took over.

> I felt myself drowning and I wanted to be with him. I had no hope for my future, just like Ryan didn't have for his.

Andrea's story echoes what many of us feel after we lose the one we love: despair and a loss of the future. It is especially tragic when death has come to a child or young adult, who had a whole life to look forward to.

But for you, there *will* be a future, even only for today. More than likely, there will be a new day after this one and one after that. Hope tells you that tomorrow might be brighter than today. Hope is the life preserver you can hold on to even when you can't see or feel any brightness; you just need to believe it is there in the darkness, awaiting your grasp. In fact, you may hold on to it most in those times when you see the least.

Andrea went on to say,

> I realized I was not going to die and there would be a future, so I had to find a way to live again. I thought that maybe there could be something to live for, maybe I would find a way through this darkness. I didn't feel it and, for a long time, I just held on to the idea—the possibility that there *could* be hope.

Hope means something is possible. Try this affirmation exercise; begin each of the following statements with *I hope*:

Things will get better.
I will feel moments of peace today.
Today may bring some good things into my life.
Life can be good.
I can make this journey.

Now add four affirmative statements of your own. For example:

I hope I can make dinner for my family today.
I hope I can find something to be happy about.
I hope I can talk to my kids/husband/family today.
I hope I can get through this day.

Use your imagination; use any theme you can think of. Type and print out these affirmations on your computer, or write them down, and put them on your bathroom mirror or someplace you can see them. The goal is to remind yourself every day that hope is a possibility, and to take advantage of its proximity to act as though it is really there . . . even if you can't see it.

Faith/Spirituality

EVEN IF YOU may have strayed from a traditional belief system, faith and spirituality are still essential qualities. When I say faith, I mean religious faith—the faith you may have grown up in or embraced as an adult. It is a formal, organized religion, with a certain set of rules, observances, and dogma.

Spirituality is the breath that makes religion alive. It brings life into the structure of rules and dogma, and gives them meaning. Without it, religion is an empty set of rigid regulations and observances. Think of spirituality as the light that comes into the house and makes it a home.

However, spirituality is also present in many other forms besides religion. For example, a person can have a strong spiritual belief in the sacredness of life, but not attend formal services. A person can have a strong link with the divine through nature and choose not to be part of an organized religion. Or a person can live a highly ethical life with no beliefs in any specific religion or even in spirituality.

Conversely, religious practice does not always mean spirituality. We can go to church, temple, or mosque every week, yet still keep the spirit out of our lives. We can observe the rules and dogma, but not embrace spirituality.

Gina, a woman whose stepson, William, was murdered, said the following:

> I considered myself to have a good faith. I went to services every Sunday; I believed in God. But I don't think I gave much thought to how this worked in my life. I didn't think God cared about me. He lived in church on Sunday. When William was murdered, I had to find him in my daily life, in the little things. Not just in church on Sunday, obeying all the rules. For a long time, I couldn't. I couldn't believe in a God that allowed the murder of young children. I had to ask myself if I truly believed. If I did, then I had to start acting like it.

Violence will test your faith in what you believe. It will demand from you a spirituality that works, one that is alive and powerful. Many, in the aftermath of so profound a loss, do not find the strength they need in their religious faith. They may be disillusioned by what has happened and abandon their faith because they believe it has abandoned them. They may feel betrayed, believing that their loved one was not protected from danger or spared from death by their guiding spirit. This is not at all abnormal but, rather, a painful and entirely reasonable reaction to what has happened.

On the other hand, many will find that it is their very faith that keeps them alive during such times. When tragedy strikes, faith becomes something real, something they actually believe in rather than something they give lip service to. These people find that the traumatic event serves to awaken or strengthen, not weaken, their beliefs.

This is your journey, not anyone else's. You cannot nor should you try to steer your way through it along someone else's course. In our world, there are many ways to find the breath of life. You must honor these differences and your fellow travelers, and leave room for what they can bring to your communal journey. Wherever you are with regard to your faith and spirituality, you deserve acknowledgement and respect. Every one of us has the freedom to choose our way, not as another would wish us to. This is not a time to let religion or the absence/diversity of it drive a wedge between yourself and friends or family. You all need to move forward, each in your own way. The next time you meet a pilgrim, acknowledge that while there are different ways to cross the ocean, you are all in this together.

RESOLVING A CRISIS IN FAITH

Faith and spirituality are powerful tools to help, not condemn or dishearten us. Teresa, whose sister, Meredith, was killed by an abusive spouse, faced this dilemma:

> I thought I had a strong faith; I knew its tenets and believed in God and that if I was good, nothing bad would happen to me or my family. Well, it did. My sister married someone who beat her and finally killed her. I was furious. How could God allow this to happen? I prayed and nothing changed. All those years I trusted him to take care of my sister and he didn't. Why did he allow this to happen? Why did he have to punish her this way? I was done with God, maybe forever.

Teresa's thinking is common for trauma survivors: if we are good, nothing bad will happen. Then, we become angry and confused when something bad *does* happen. Our experience forces us to work through this paradox. We realize that being good is not a guarantee of a long or perfect life.

When Aaron was murdered, people said to me, "How could God do this to him?" It never occurred to me that God murdered Aaron. Two men did. In my belief system, God does not murder, but *people* do it all the time: that is human nature. I did not come to this understanding easily; it took years to develop the concept of a loving God and the fact that people do these terrible things, not

God. This was a quality of my faith and spirituality I already had when Aaron was killed. It was tortuously tested by his murder and many times I continue to wonder how human beings can do such awful things to one another.

In the introduction to his book *When Bad Things Happen to Good People*, Rabbi Harold Kushner says, "This can't be happening, this is not how the world is supposed to work. Tragedies were supposed to happen to selfish, dishonest people—how could this be happening to me?" The truth is that bad things *do* happen to good people. Bad things happen to bad people, too. In other words, bad things happen to *everyone*, not because God has it out for us, or that we are bad or good, but because that is the nature of life.

THE AFTERLIFE

One of the great gifts of religion and spiritual traditions is a set of beliefs about the afterlife. If you believe there is a life after death, this can be a valuable, important inner resource, one that brings comfort and a sense that the one you love still lives, albeit in a different form.

On the day of Aaron's funeral, I remembered how, when he was born, the midwife cut the umbilical cord. On the morning of the funeral, I felt the unseen cord that always connected us hanging there, lifeless. Now that he is gone, the spirit of the cord between us searches for him; I can feel the cord trying to reconnect with him wherever he is. Surely this speaks to the bond between mother and child, a bond that is so strong, it can never be broken, not even in death. This experience not only strengthened my belief in the afterlife, but challenged me to live in both the physical and the spiritual world. In the years since his death, the cord has indeed stretched far and wide.

In July 1999, two months after Aaron's death, I was sitting on the beach in New Jersey. I was looking out on the blue waters, just like they were when I was a child. I took the kids here when they were younger; I recalled Aaron playing in the sand . . . his hair, bleached blond by the sun. I began crying because he was gone; I couldn't believe his senseless murder had happened. Then I became aware of someone next to me. I looked; it was Aaron, tall, healthy, tanned, a beautiful vision, unlike the horror of what had happened to him.

He said, "Mom, I'm so happy!" I looked at him and cried, "How can you be happy without us?" "I miss you so much, son." Then, he said again: "Mom, I'm so happy." He stayed with me awhile until I felt at peace.

While I was glad for him, I missed him so much. I wanted him back. Yet, I was comforted by his visit. I was grateful that he was still alive in his own way and most of all that he was happy.

Whether this vision was "real" or not is irrelevant. My beliefs gave me a connection with my son in the afterlife and that is what I needed. I have nurtured that belief in the years since his death.

What are your beliefs in the afterlife, and how do those beliefs serve you? Do you have dreams or a sense of your loved one's presence? If you do, these are an important and profound part of your story and can be written about or shared, or made a part of your journal. Honor them as gifts of the spirit—things to hold on to when you miss the one you love so much that you feel like giving up.

IT IS ENTIRELY normal that, in your grief, you will feel your faith and spirituality are being tested. You are face to face with a challenge to understand and live what you believe. You are fully entitled in your humanity to question, become angry, feel abandoned. The turbulence of your emotions may cause you to reexamine everything you thought you believed, and will force you to do the hard work of deciding what, in fact, you do believe. When you emerge from this struggle, you will be that much stronger for it, more so than if you took comfort in a blind faith you did not really understand.

After his wife's murder in a random robbery, Ron's faith was challenged and renewed. He tells us his story:

> When Deb was murdered, all of my beliefs were challenged. Yes, I went to temple (more for Debra and the

kids), and I *said* I believed. But when it came time to back it up, I couldn't. There wasn't anything there but anger and disbelief for a very long time. I didn't have much use for God, since it seemed like he was too cruel to take my wife away from me and the kids.

Then one day, my daughter Rachel, who was five, asked if mommy was with God. I said I didn't know. She said to me, "But mommy has to be somewhere, and that must be where she is." My daughter in her simple logic was right. Deb has to be somewhere, and if that's true, she must be with God.

Sometimes the simpler the faith, the easier it is to understand. Whatever your beliefs, ask yourself if you actually believe them. For example, if your faith tells you there is a life after death, do you believe that? Do you believe you will see your loved one again? If you do, allow that faith to comfort you and help you.

If you feel you have lost your faith, have tolerance for yourself; condemn neither yourself nor the religion. Rather than discarding them wholesale, reconsider the individual aspects of your former beliefs and see if any still hold comfort for you. If not, ask yourself if there is something else of a spiritual nature that still brings you comfort. For example, it could be the blessings of the life you shared with the one you loved, or the gifts that person brought into your life.

Remember to exercise kindness toward yourself. Realize that sorting out your faith and spirituality is a process, one that takes time. Your beliefs will go through many changes over the years.

Optimism

BEFORE AARON'S MURDER, I thought of the world as a good place. While it might have had lots of things to worry about, my perception was that basically, it was a hospitable place, full of both good and bad. I had an optimistic view of the world; although I had tremendous fears about the glass being half empty, I knew that it could also be half full, and half full felt better.

When asked about her worldview, whether it was optimistic or pessimistic, Barbara, of whom I spoke earlier, said the following:

> I never really thought about it. I suppose I thought the world was not a particularly good place. I think, in retrospect, I saw the world as a scary place, one that didn't care much about me. I just wanted to live my life quietly, and control everything. The house, the picket fence, the perfect family, that was all so that I didn't have to think of the world as bad. I believed I could protect myself from it and therefore only good things would happen.

Barbara discovered that, in her worldview, she believed the glass was half empty. She recognized that she felt uncomfortable in the world, that it was full of land mines that would go off if she stepped on one. Therefore, when she was young, she decided it was better to create a safe place where she could control what happened. After Steven's death, she realized that, in many ways, she had always been pessimistic, and that this pessimism was turning into hatred for the world that took her husband. Barbara was being swallowed up by a world she despised. She knew this attitude was killing her:

> I can't live this way. I want to live in a world that isn't full of horror. I want to have a place in the world. I want to able to wake up and say, yes, there is horror in the world, but there are good things, too.

For Barbara, that meant recognizing that she could change the way she *thought* about the world. It wasn't a place that wanted to hurt her but, rather, one in which hurtful things may sometimes—not always—happen. She used the quality of optimism to help her change her worldview and see the world as a good place.

I had to reconcile Aaron's brutal murder with the world I knew and loved. I began to think maybe my view of the world was naïve and that, in fact, it was a cruel, terrible place. Maybe I had been too optimistic previously, and needed more pessimism—and, therefore, I began to let the world take on a terrible, cynical twist. But, like Barbara, I didn't want to live in a world like that. Yes, I knew there would still be instances of cruelty, of terror. But I did not want to be further victimized by allowing those things to destroy my view of the world. That would betray the memory of Aaron and everything we as a family stood for.

The questions life asks us are these: Can we, despite our tragedies, in spite of the horror in the world, still believe it is a good place? Can we either maintain our general optimism or learn to develop it, after disaster strikes? Ask yourself those questions. Try and understand your worldview and see where you can change it, even slightly, to be more optimistic. I don't expect you to suddenly see everything in a rosy glow. What I am asking you to do is look at the world with a willingness to see it in a better light. What happened may have cast a strong shadow of terror; the world seems irrevocably changed, hostile, threatening. But if you can develop a willing attitude to balance your view with optimism, it will help you. If you can embrace this viewpoint, you will begin to see that what you have experienced is part of the world, but not all of it. Overall, the world is still a good place.

A greeting card printed some years ago and one which a good friend sent to me read, "Barn burnt down; now I can see the moon." One way to encourage a more positive outlook would be to simply take a walk. Look for sights and sounds of life. It may be a bird singing, a sunrise or sunset, a flower or a lovely tree that catches your attention. The world is still here, with all its beauty and uplifting elements; allow yourself to take it in. Or, think of a time when the world gave you something beautiful and hold that memory close to you.

Humor

HUMOR MAY SEEM like a tall order here; there is surely nothing funny about violence. Yet, there can be humor in the way we look at things. When we were standing at Aaron's gravesite, the day of the funeral, a bird flew by and a splat landed on the coffin. My cousin, Joy, said, "It's good luck!" One of the young people exclaimed, "Oh, Aaron!" An automatic laugh came out of me; I smiled because that is just the sort of irreverent thing that Aaron would do. In the middle of the something serious, he would always find a way to make it lighter.

When Laura's sister, Tory, committed suicide, she lost the dry sense of humor she had been known for. Nothing was funny for a long time. She realized she needed some laughter to help her get through that awful time. She went to the video store and rented funny movies, watched them, and allowed herself to laugh again. She said,

> I felt guilty about laughing again. How could I think something was funny when my sister took her own life?—I thought people would think I was shallow or maybe didn't take her death seriously. The truth was, I took it so seriously, I wanted to die, too. But I also wanted to survive and I needed that thing I always had—the ability to laugh. I realized, too, that Tory always loved my sense of humor; she used to say it made her feel better. So I started laughing *for* her, telling her little jokes—it made me feel better.

Honor the memory of the one you love by keeping your sense of humor and remembering theirs. Celebrate their lives by doing some things that are fun and things they would like you to do. Maybe that means something as simple as renting a funny movie they liked and watching it.

There are studies that prove laughter is healthy—so maybe it's true that laughter is the best medicine. We all need reprieve from the burden we carry, even if just for a moment. Open yourself to humor—indeed, try to find it wherever you can. Remember that, even in the depth of sorrow, there can be the lightness to our humanity. I am reminded of the two faces we often see associated with drama: tragedy and comedy. Perhaps they give us a way to look at life: they are two sides of the same face, one happy, one tragic. One does not exist without the other. The challenge is to allow ourselves to feel both.

Your journey cannot always be full of the awful things that happened; you would sink beneath the weight of that. You need to balance your tragedy with the literal lightness of humor. So, today, think of a funny story and laugh, tell a joke, or call someone and remind them of something funny you both remember. It is not disrespectful of the dead to raise your own spirits.

Patience

PATIENCE IS ONE of those qualities that some possess in great measure, but others, like me, have to work at. During those first days in Steubenville, I found myself agitated and impatient at everything that was going on. Why couldn't they find out where Aaron and Brian were? I felt the clock ticking to find them; little did I know they were already dead. During the trial, I was impatient with our legal system and just about everything that was happening. Most of all, I was impatient with my grief. It hurt so much all the time, I just wanted it to be over. I had to learn to be patient with my suffering and not allow my impatience to spill out on everyone and everything.

In our hectic world, we race to do everything; patience seems to be left by the roadside. Yet we need it in almost everything we do and we need it with others. You especially need it now, on this journey. There is nothing that will hurry things along. The process will unfold at its own pace. The gift patience gives to you, if you allow it, is a modicum of peace within all this turbulence—an oasis of calm.

There is an old story about a woman who was trying to climb a wall in the hot sun. She wanted desperately to climb it and tried everything. She pushed, she complained, she beat the wall, but still, she could not climb it. She only exhausted herself in the blazing sun. Finally, she sat against the wall, under the shade of a tree, and rested. Later, in the cool of the evening, her strength was restored. She looked at the wall again more slowly, carefully. And then she discovered there was a path around the wall.

Nina tells the following story:

> When my husband, Gary, was assaulted and nearly killed, he was left disabled, frightened, and unable to care for himself. I tried, I really did, but I kept losing my patience with him. I wanted him back the way he was, strong, capable of taking care of things. I was not doing well at all—I realized I would have to develop better patience if both of us were to survive. I did and what this has taught me is something I never had—patience and peace.

In your life, look and see in what areas you need to develop patience. Try a small experiment: when you are aware of something or someone that you are impatient with, slow down, stop pushing, take a deep breath, and let nature run its course. You may be surprised to find that the situation resolves itself anyway, without any need for urgency or effort. Look at it this way: You are already feeling overwhelmed by circumstances you have not been able to do anything to prevent. Why create stress for yourself in areas you *can* control?

Joy

At dusk weeping comes for the night, but Joy
cometh in the morning.

—PSALM 30

JOY IS AN elusive quality, one everyone seems to want but few
people have. Often, joy comes only after the struggle, not before. It
is not something you can buy or borrow, but rather something that
comes directly out of pain and sorrow. Joy is the sister of hope. Joy
follows the long labor of childbirth; it is springtime after the harsh
winter and eternity after the brief breath of life.

As these verses from the Old Testament, in the Book of Lam-
entations, 15–18, tell us:

> Joy has vanished from our hearts;
> Our dancing has turned to mourning
> Our hearts are sick; our eyes are dim
> Because mount Zion is desolate
> Jackals roam to and fro on it

For those of us who have survived the violent death of someone
we love, the jackals indeed roam. Our lives are desolate and our
hearts are sick. How can we be joyful when such awful things have
happened to us and those we love?

An even greater tragedy would be to allow violence to keep us
from joy; then truly, it has destroyed us. Even if you do not feel joy
now, believe that, in the future it will come, if you allow it.

Try this exercise: Imagine yourself sometime in the future. You
wake up and go to your window. When you look outside, you see the
sun coming up. It's radiant. There are colors of soft blues and gray,
and the morning star sparkles. It's going to be a clear, beautiful day,

more beautiful than anything you have seen in a long time. You feel a long-forgotten feeling—it's joy! You smile and realize it has come back again, if only for a moment, in a mental projection.

There are many ways to remind yourself of joy. One simple way is to recall a memory. I'll share one of mine with you. It happened when I lived in the mountains of Colorado. It was June, a few months before I was to return to Philadelphia. I was sitting outside and, to my complete amazement, I saw tiny hummingbirds flying over the flowers I had planted. Their shimmering feathers of blue and green were vibrating as they drew nectar from the pink and purple flowers.

This was a rare sight, especially in such high elevations and long, cold winters. The birds came for several days, and I looked forward to seeing them. I knew that in Native American spiritual traditions, the hummingbird symbolizes joy. This was a gift I continued to remember, even in my darkest hours when joy seemed gone forever.

Linda's story also emphasizes what memories can bring us:

> When Sam, my son, was killed, how could I feel joy? Joy in what? All of his future was taken from him and me. But when the second birthday after his death came, I was thinking about his birth and what he was like as a baby. I felt joy in remembering what I did have with him. No one or no thing could ever rob me of that memory and that joy. I would hold on to those memories like gold—they were my treasures; they brought me joy.

You will have your own memories of joyful times shared with your loved one. Summon to your consciousness one of those memories. Record it in your journal, tell it to someone, smile to yourself about it, and keep it close to mind and heart. You do homage to your loved one when you remember to feel joy in your life. It will survive even the strongest storm, if you allow it to. If there is no joy in the everyday, look again to your memories. Those moments were real, and therefore remain real. No one and nothing can take those from you. Use them to lighten your burden and light your way.

Compassion

COMPASSION PERHAPS IS the most profound gift your sorrow and suffering can give to you. Buddhists call compassion the jewel of suffering—it comes directly out of one's pain. When you fully experience the depth of your sorrow, your heart opens. You are able to see and understand the suffering of others because now you, too, have suffered deeply. Once you have known sorrow, you can empathize, not just sympathize, with others and truly be with them. You can offer your help because you know what helped you—and what did not.

Remember to develop compassion for yourself first. This means to truly be present for your own feelings, not dismissing or repressing them. These feelings bring you into the human family: it is here we all meet—not in the shallow surfaces of life, but in the deep experiences that make us reach out for one another. When this happens, you begin to think less of what your needs are and more of what you can do to help someone else.

At first, you may not be able to think of helping others, so great is your own pain. This is natural, yet compassion will come to you if you open yourself to it. When you offer your experience to others, it will help you. This is the great paradox of suffering: to reach out in compassion to another helps one's own self. How? If you change the focus from yourself to others, for that time, you forget about your pain and feel better. In this manner, you find meaning to your suffering and bring something valuable out of it. Many kinds of support organizations have helped countless people in pain following a tragedy or struggling with disabilities, precisely because one person undergoing the experience reached out to offer comfort. You could be the one person to turn someone else's life around, even while you are still seeking resolution for your own grief, and you will feel so much better for it.

In recounting her story, Valerie said,

> When my son Devon was killed in a drive-by shooting, I was paralyzed with grief; then I began to realize that other people suffered, too. I reached out to other parents whose children had been murdered. I knew what they were experiencing—I could help them, and it actually helped me get out of myself—this was an unexpected gift but one that helped me as much as it helped them.

Think about how your experience can help another. You know now what it is like to lose someone to violence. You may not be able to do something for someone else today, but there may come an opportunity for you to open your heart.

Meanwhile, you need to always remember to have compassion for your own great suffering. Recognize this is a task most of us have little or no preparation for. When tragedy blindsides us, we expect things of ourselves that we cannot do—like getting "back to normal" or "getting over it."

Understand that true compassion comes out of the grief you first feel for yourself; allow it to make you human—like everyone else. As Viktor Frankl said,

> We who lived in concentration camps can remember the men who walked through the huts comforting others, giving away their last piece of bread. They may have been few in number, but they offer sufficient proof that everything can be taken from a man but one thing: the last of the human freedoms—to choose one's attitude in any given set of circumstances, to choose one's own way.

Putting It All Together

COURAGE, HOPE, FAITH/SPIRITUALITY, optimism, humor, patience, joy, and compassion help you to do what life asks of you—to survive this journey and live again. They will help you make your suffering work for you, to allow it to transform rather than destroy you. Be patient with yourself as you learn to use these eight qualities; it will take time to cross the ocean and reclaim your world from being the dark place it is now to one that is filled with promise and good. And remember that you, too, have the last of the human freedoms—to choose your own way.

Stage 3

Lighthouses in the Harbor

FINDING GUIDANCE AND RESOURCES

N O ONE SHOULD carry this terrible burden alone. Even the strongest among us asks for help along the way. We fall, and someone helps us until we are strong enough to begin again.

In stage 2, you became acquainted with your life preservers, which will help you bear the weight of your story and transform your suffering. Stage 3 will help you build a network of guidance and good resources to call upon for relief, support, and care. Although you may feel stranded and alone, you are fortunate in that there are many resources available to enable you to build a strong network, which like lighthouses in the harbor will guide you when the way seems dark and overwhelming, and the ocean too deep to cross. These include:

Personal Resources
+ Family
+ Pets
+ Friends
+ Co-workers

Community Resources
+ Community support groups
+ Victims services

Therapies
+ Psychological
+ Hypnotherapy
+ Group therapy
+ Medical
+ Holistic mind/body
+ Spiritual
+ Art
+ Nature

You can use any or all of these resources, depending on what you need, what is available, and what makes sense to you. Your needs may change over time; some of these resources may be needed only as temporary aides; others may become a welcome part of your daily life because you find pleasure as well as solace in them. Keep an open mind; some of these resources may be new to you, yet they may prove to be quite helpful. A detailed list of resources also appears in the appendix.

Personal Resources

WHEN A PERSONAL tragedy occurs, it is natural to feel overwhelmed by, or to not even be able to focus upon, building extensive resources. You will more likely turn to your immediate family or friends for help.

Perhaps, in your particular circumstance, close relatives are already involved and are experiencing the event with you. They may include a spouse, significant other, or children. Perhaps this circle may also include parents, siblings grandparents, aunts, uncles, or cousins; your own close friends, or people who were otherwise close to the deceased, such as girlfriends or boyfriends, old or current roommates, or workplace colleagues. You will all be giving support to one another as the trauma unfolds; the chances are, no one will have all the facts or be supremely organized at coping with them. At this point, numbness, disbelief, and disorganization will prevail.

Unlike losses that unfold at a more "natural" pace (such as death through illness) murder and violence are immediate and horrifying, not only because of the instant impact, but because of the nature of the crime—someone taking or altering the life of yourself or someone you love. No one is ever prepared for such an event—and afterward, family members and close friends are often unable to support one another because of the extreme shock each one is facing. Some may cling to one another trying to find their way, while others may avoid personal contact because it is just too painful to be reminded of their loss. Sometimes the focus of everybody becomes dealing with the externals in a mechanical fashion, because the full depth of their grief has not yet hit them.

For example, while we were in Steubenville searching for Aaron and Brian, my family and Brian's traveled as though we were a single family, all with one end: to stay together and support one another while we tried to find the missing boys. I realized later that so much of my response was automatic. I was in shock, and so was everyone else. We seemed to exist in a kind of floating world, holding on to whatever was left of our lives. We did whatever was in front of us, on autopilot, like robots—going to and from the police station, the university, and the hotel. It was only later that I could think more clearly about what could be done for Anna and Michael, me, and everyone else involved.

It may seem overwhelming even to imagine how your family and friends might be able to help you. Here is an exercise to simplify the thought process. Turn on the computer, or sit down with a pen and paper, and write yourself two lists:

- ✦ Which relatives/friends may I reliably approach for support?
- ✦ What do I need done by these people?

The first question is usually pretty easy. You know to whom you can go versus who would probably be less helpful. This is not the time to try to change an ungiving person's nature or strive to patch up a pretrauma relationship merely to get something from that person; if you already know you will receive rejection or an apathetic response, reach for someone you *know* will be there for you. But don't slam the door: trauma can also bring people together—you may be surprised by who will help when you least expect it. When her son was killed, Valerie found a new source of support when her mainstay was unavailable:

> My mother was a source of strength to me throughout my life. However, when Devon was killed, she was ill. I talked to her—but I also knew that she was sick and therefore I did not want to lean on her as much as before. I was lucky; my sister stepped up and said she would be there for me whatever I needed.

The second question may be more difficult. When a tragedy occurs, everyone has different needs. Here are some things you may need:

+ Comfort, support, to be listened to
+ Help making the funeral arrangements or doctor/therapy appointments
+ Help with food, laundry, cleaning, or errands
+ Help with phone calls or getting documents, death certificates, etc.
+ Help learning about and settling the deceased person's business/personal affairs
+ Help dealing with the person's belongings or pets
+ Protection from intrusive people
+ Hands-on care for such members of the household as babies or small children, disabled persons, or elderly parents
+ Financial help

That last may be the hardest to request, but swallow your pride and ask for it—or just be thankful and accept it should it be offered. When Aaron was murdered, I was confronted with many unexpected events, not the least of which was the funeral and its expenses. My family knew this, and tried to help where they could. My brothers assumed some of the expenses and, when my aunt and uncle found out, they came forward to offer a plot they already owned at the cemetery where many of my family members are buried. This was a kind and generous gift to me, one which I would not have even thought of asking for.

Many people will want to come forward and help. If you can, let them know what you need, using the above list as a guide, instead of leaving them to intuit how they might be most useful. Or, give your list to someone who can organize people willing to help. If it is hard for you to think straight just now, ask a trusted friend or family member to draw up your list of probable needs, review it, and then let that person administer it.

 ### *What Can I Do to Help? I Don't Know What to Say.*

IF YOU WISH to offer help to a friend or relative, look at the following list, think about what you could do, and offer a specific service to the person or his/her family. It could be something as simple as taking over their dog-walking while the family attends to more urgent business . . . or as heartwrenching as helping a bereaved parent select burial garments. Whatever you can do, volunteer assistance without waiting to be asked; and if a person close to the deceased assigns you a task, do it without complaint or squeamishness. These are extraordinary times, and even a small act of kindness or practicality might mean the world to the recipient.

There are many things you can do to help:

- Simply be there. Let the person know you are there for whatever he/she needs. Just your quiet presence may be

supportive if the person needs to talk or feels intimidated
by necessary discussions with professionals connected with
the case.

- A vague, general offer of assistance, such as "What can I do?"
  may be too difficult for the person to respond to, if he/she is
  feeling overwhelmed by so much needing to be done. Be as
  specific as possible, for example: "Do you need groceries?"
  or "Do you need a ride to . . . ?" or "You haven't sat down
  for hours; please, let me do that for you, and you—just rest.
  Here's a cup of tea; now, sit!"

- Don't wait for the person to call you. Be proactive; grieving
  people feel isolated and lonely, particularly after the first wave
  of the trauma has passed. Often, they will not reach out—do
  call and check up on them.

- Tell the person you are available to talk about what happened
  at any time—and really be there. Offer your shoulder to cry
  on, open your heart to the pain. This is perhaps the greatest
  gift—to listen, to encourage the person to talk rather than to
  hold the story inside.

What may not be useful:

- Saying, "It's God's will." People may conclude this eventually
  because of their own faith, but it is not a scenario to impose
  upon them while they are still reeling from the shock of a
  violent death.

- Being overly sentimental; for example, declaring the loved one
  is in heaven, happy, and so on.

- Telling a bereaved parent he or she will have more children.

- Telling the person you know what he or she is going through
  (you don't, unless you, too, have experienced the *exact* same
  thing).

- Asking for details, unless the person is clearly willing to tell
  you the story.

What may be useful:

- Share a wonderful memory that you have of that person, or express how much he or she cared for the one who is grieving.
- Offer photographs or other special mementos of the person to the family, who may not have something current of that nature.
- If you are not part of the most immediate family, *immediately* send the closest member to the deceased a note of condolence, however brief, written in your own words, rather than just signing an impersonal store-bought card. This is especially important if you are not able to be there in person. It may seem like a trivial act, but is in fact incredibly impactful; people even in the deepest shock or despair usually recall for many years and with absolute precision, who spoke out to comfort them and who did not.

The best thing is to not run away—try to stay with the grieving person through even aspects that make you sick or afraid, though seeing sides of him or her that perhaps you have never known before. You are not obligated or genuinely may not be able to fix or change every circumstance affecting the person; just be there to help in whatever way you *can* be of assistance.

FAMILY

Every family has its own configuration of members. Even when these configurations appear to be similar, the members have different relationships with one another, ranging from close to distant, amicable to antagonistic. You may have family members who live nearby and are willing to help, others may be more distant physically or emotionally. Even if you have experienced the loss of someone related to them, you may not be able to call upon them to help you through this event.

How people support one another in such a situation will have
a lot to do with their preexisting relationships. Trauma can either
bring the family closer or exacerbate existing difficulties, sometimes
in unexpected ways. Ron said,

> When Debra was murdered, we were in such shock; we
> traveled together like refugees from a war. My children
> could not sleep alone. Deb's parents were older and
> the shock almost killed them. I thought I would have
> to protect them but, instead, we all took care of each
> other. We all stayed together for the first weeks, so we
> could help each other. We had always had a good family
> relationship; now we became closer than ever before.

Remember that close family members are experiencing this
terrible event in their own way, which may be very different from
your way. Have respect for each other's way of doing things and try
to talk openly about the feelings you are having, respectfully, kindly.
Do not just assume things without discussing them; be you numb or
reeling with emotion, you may be misinterpreting what others are
thinking or feeling, and they, you. For example, Andrea said,

> After Ryan committed suicide, I couldn't face my hus-
> band, Thomas. I felt like he thought it was my fault.
> I felt like I couldn't call on him for support—there
> were problems before Ryan's death, and they just got
> worse.

Andrea assumed her husband was angry with her, which led
her to behave toward him in a certain way that proved even more
alienating. But when she was able to bring herself to sit down with
Thomas to talk about her feelings, she discovered that he thought
that *she* blamed *him*—and he hadn't been able face her!

After a violent death, the problems that may develop or

exacerbate between spouses can be devastating to the relationship. It is important for the two of you to talk about your feelings to one another. You may wish to say to your spouse, "I know this is so hard for us. Let's find time to sit down and talk about what we are both feeling, maybe we can help each other." Then set a time. If your spouse does not want to talk, suggest that he/she at least listen to what you have to say. When you share with each other, avoid the following:

- Blame
- Accusations
- Assumptions

Instead, say to him/her:

- "This is the way I feel about . . ."
- "I am having trouble with . . ."
- "Can you help me, and tell me what you are feeling, thinking, about . . ."

This may be difficult. Not everyone wants to talk about their feelings, but the idea here is to create an opportunity for your family members to express themselves and for you to clarify some of the things you may be feeling or thinking about them or others. Use this rule of thumb: When in doubt, ask the person; do not assume what he/she is thinking, feeling, or doing. Above all, try not to blame the person for what happened, or for emotional reactions that are different from your own. Remember, you haven't experienced this before, and neither have the other members of your family. A person who does not show outward signs of grieving, for instance, may still be in tremendous pain. Likewise, someone already burdened with other difficulties may truly be unable to offer much assistance to you, even in this extreme circumstance. Relatives may be too devastated to be able to help you . . . can you rise above this and help them?

PETS

A special note here about the four-footed, finned, or feathered members of our families. Often, it is our pets that bring us comfort and solace. They can love us in a way that humans often cannot. As Maya shared,

> I had always loved horses; my father taught me to ride when I was a little girl. After he was murdered, I would ride Champ out in the fields, sometimes furiously fast, other times slow and steady. When we rested, I would cry and he would come over and nuzzle me and I would hold on to him. I would always feel better after our ride.

There are many stories of how our animals brought love into our lives and stayed with us during the darkest times, when no one else was there. If you have such a family member, its love may be good therapy for you. And, likewise, your loved one's pet may also be experiencing a devastating sense of loss and confusion, particularly if surrounded by a family clearly in panic or pain, and be in need of comfort and reassurance. Soothe a pet as you would a frightened child, and you will both feel better for it. If you are not up to making arrangements for a pet's care, add this to your list for someone else to take over that responsibility as quickly as possible.

FRIENDS

Unfortunately, some important family members may not be able to help each other. Perhaps they don't live nearby, have passed away, or are estranged. Their absence at such a time be a sorrowful thing to experience, compounding the grief you already feel. If this is the case, you will need to broaden your support network. For many people, it is their friends who help them through trauma. Even one friend can make a difference. As Barbara, about whom I told you earlier, said,

> I lost my parents in a car accident when I was young. I did have my grandmother, but she was elderly and I was worried about her health. I didn't want to burden her. But I did have a close friend; we knew each other since childhood. I trusted her, and she was there for me when it happened and, as much as she could help, she did.

 ### If You Are a Friend of Someone Who Has Lost a Loved One to Violence

IF YOUR FRIEND does ask to be alone, give consideration to that—but call to see if he or she is all right. Just letting the person know you are there can help.

The telephone can keep you connected. Perhaps you can arrange for a daily check-in, a few minutes in the morning to start the day. You may also use e-mail to keep in touch with your friend; by that means, the person will be able to access (and reread) what you have to say, and respond, whenever he or she wishes, in a less pressured way than using the phone. However you choose to keep in touch, remember that, for a person in crisis, knowing someone is thinking about you and wants to help can make a difference.

CO-WORKERS

After the initial trauma has passed, you may return to work. This, of course, is a challenge to you and the people you work with. You will want to resume your responsibilities, yet you will obviously be under continued obligations involving or emotionally distracted by what has happened to you. Finding balance is no easy task. If you have a supportive environment, people will try to help you, but they, too, will be adjusting and might not know what to do, either. It would be wise to discuss coming back to work with your boss or human resources person. Tell him or her what you think you can do, what you think you can't do (at least for the time being), and what you need. Here are some examples of things to negotiate:

+ To work on a part-time basis
+ To work with the caveat you may need to reduce your schedule/ work load
+ To suggest returning on a trial basis to see what you are able to do
+ To accomplish some of your work from home, such as via a net-worked computer or company-funded phone tie-line, to enable you to also devote time to necessities within your household

There is no rule for when to return to work. You may not have a choice; you may have to return as soon as you are able, or following a set period of days for mourning permitted by a corporation. This is particularly true for men and women who are the full-time breadwinners in their households. In any case, ask your human resources person or your employer up front what policies are in place for personal absences, sick time, vacations, sabbaticals, and so on, and see if you can negotiate to draw upon the total time available to you. Ask if taking an unpaid leave with a definite date set for your return would be a viable means of keeping your job, should you have too few days of paid leave to remain absent.

Many people report that when they feel they are ready to go back to work, they actually like the distraction that work can offer. Melanie, whose fiancé was shot in a random burglary, said,

> When Michael was murdered, I took a leave of absence from work. After two months, I decided to go back to work part-time. Although it was really hard, I found that it brought me some relief to think of something else.

I do want to caution you against returning to work right away as, though things will be "normal," they will not be for you. You will need to allow space and time for your grief. Even if you think you are okay, talk about how you feel about returning to the workplace, where you may experience stresses or an impersonal setting that you coped with fine previously, but which may now overwhelm you. Here is where you can use the help of a therapist, clergy member, family, and friends, to analyze the nature of your workplace and your own readiness to return to it. If you do decide to go to work, it may be helpful to meet with a few of the people you work closely with, and run by them what you think you might need. They could be a good barometer of how workplace sentiment may greet your arrival—if they show any awkwardness toward you, it tells you that colleagues with whom you have even less of a personal relationship may be unsure about how it will be to work with you now. For example, you might say to an office mate, "I'm coming back to work but don't know what it's going to like, so please bear with me. I might ask you for help—is that okay?"

Your workplace will necessitate telling your story to at least one or a few individuals. It will be important for you to tailor a version to tell these people—one that tells them what happened, but is short and protects you from intrusive comments or feeling strong emotions every time you have to speak it. Please refer back to stage 1 and read the section on tailoring your story to suit particular situations.

You may not be able to return to work for a while, or may even decide to quit your job because you just cannot return. Many changes may happen in the wake of a trauma, not the least of which may affect your ability or desire to go to work. If you are able to, take some time off and decide what you want to be doing; the important thing is to resist doing anything sudden that you may regret and not be able to reconstruct. When in doubt, tread water, without yet turning away from this familiar landmark of your old life. Once you arrive at the other shore of your journey, you may decide more calmly and thoughtfully on an entirely different choice of work.

IF ONE OF your co-workers has lost someone to violence, you can help by doing the following:

- Don't tiptoe around as if there is something wrong with the person.
- Don't assume the person does or doesn't want to talk about it.
- Don't say trite and sentimental things, such as "Time heals all wounds," or "It was God's will."
- Don't avoid the person.

Instead, be honest, and say or do something like:

- I don't know what to say, but if you want to talk, I'm here.
- I know this must be tough; if you need anything, please ask me, I'll do whatever I can.
- I am so sorry. I'm here if you need anything

If you see your co-worker is overwhelmed by workplace responsibilities (without perching over the person's shoulder or pronouncing judgments, such as, "Boy, you're really out of it today."), ask him or her if you can help. Make it casual, and don't demand reciprocity.

Ask the person if he or she would like to go out after work or join some of you for a quiet dinner or lunch. If he or she doesn't want to, don't take it personally; just say, "Fine, let's do it another time," and don't forget to ask later, after a few weeks have gone by. The workplace and colleagues may feel very foreign now to your co-worker; don't nag that he or she join you for non-work-related social activities you used to enjoy together (lunches, birthday parties, sports events, and so on) but don't exclude the person or assume one no means always no, either. Invite your co-worker to join you on a case-by-case basis, and let the person decide whether he or she feels up to socializing. Don't take it as a personal slight if the answer is no; leave the door open for an eventual yes.

Community Resources

COMMUNITY SUPPORT GROUPS

There are community groups that offer counseling and support for families of victims of violent crimes. These are funded privately, through members, or through the government, and are free of charge.

Following are the names and Web sites of several support groups I am familiar with; you can find more information on the Web by using in a search engine such keywords and phrases as "victims support" or "community groups victims violent crime." Also, the appendix at the back of this book contains additional resources.

+ *Parents of Murdered Children*, www.pomc.com, is a valuable resource dedicated to families who have lost children to murder, whatever their ages. After all, everyone who has been murdered is someone's child. They are a strong voice for survivors and victims. They offer support at parole hearings as well as support groups in our communities. They help us keep the memories of our children alive and offer many resources from those who actually have experienced what many of us are going through.
+ *Surviving Suicide*, www.survivingsuicide.com, is a Web site for healing after the loss of a loved one by suicide. It offers good information, plus links to many other sites that can help you find resources and support. Suicide, like all other forms of violence, has its own particular and devastating grief for those who survive the loss of a loved one. This website and other community groups can assist you in finding help.
+ *Compassionate Friends*, www.compassionatefriends.org, is for people who have lost children, although not specifically through murder. Parents, siblings, and grandparents, as well as extended family members, are encouraged to attend support group meetings. They offer compassion and understanding, and have wonderful ways of keeping the spirit of our family members alive while honoring them.

✦ *Families of Murder Victims*, www.avpphila.org, is an organization that helps by providing counseling for family members, and
is part of the antiviolence partnership, a local organization here
in Philadelphia. After Aaron died, I met Deborah Spungen,
who started Families of Murder Victims. This was a valuable
resource for me and my children. I felt I could talk to the counselors there because they understood what happens after violent
crime. There are similar organizations in other communities.
Contact your district attorney's office to learn what's available
in your area.

VICTIMS SERVICES

Lethal, violent crimes are different than other traumas, not only
because of their brutality, but because they almost always involve
the legal system. You may have encountered the legal system in
one form or another, but this situation is something entirely new
and traumatizing. Violent crime brings with it the added burden
of dealing with police, detectives, judges and juries, and the pub-
licity the crime may generate. It requires special expertise to help
you navigate this baffling system and you should enlist whatever
assistance is available.

The person who will help you navigate the legal system is called
a "victim's advocate," and is trained to help families of crime victims
deal with not only the legal system, but also to offer guidance to other
resources that may help crime victims and their families. You can
find out if your community has a victim's advocate by calling your
district attorney's office and inquiring. If such professionals are not
available, the office may be able to recommend other services.

When Aaron was murdered, I had to learn how to deal with
the legal system. It was very difficult to feel on the outside of the
machinery of the law—not knowing what was going to happen.
I didn't know where to turn for help, but thankfully there were
programs such as these that helped me through the maze. At the
trials of Terrell Yarbrough and Nathan Herring, the men accused

of murdering Aaron, I met Teresa Laman from the prosecutor's office in Steubenville, Ohio. She helped me navigate the mystery of the court system and the trials, which were truly horrible events but made easier by Teresa's guidance. Later, I met Linda Burkett, a tireless advocate for victim's rights in the Camden, New Jersey, prosecutor's office. Thanks to her and Teresa and many others, we did not have to face the legal system alone and unrepresented. It will be a good day when every prosecutor's office has a victim's assistance program.

There is also the issue of the financial strain that may occur as a result of violent crime. For example, you may be faced with unexpected funeral expenses, may have to take time off from work, or need to handle the victim's medical costs.

There is help for these expenses. Crime victim compensation provides greatly needed financial assistance for crime victims. The first compensation program in the United States was created in California in 1965. Today, all fifty states, plus the District of Columbia and the Virgin Islands, have compensation programs. You can ask your victims advocate or inquire at your district attorney's office for information about the program in your state.

The following are a few of the national organizations that can also help you find resources and support. You can also search the Web, using the keyphrase "national organizations for victims of crime."

+ *National Organization of Victims Assistance (NOVA)*, www. trynova.org, is an organization that provides referrals, crisis counseling, and case advocacy for victims and survivors of violent crime. They sponsor a National Victims Rights week and established the first national hotline for crime victims in 1975, called the National Crime Victims Information and Referral Hotline (1-800-TRY NOVA). They frequently receive calls from victims and survivors who have no other place to turn. They are a good source of information and guidance for both victims and survivors.

+ *The Victims' Assistance Legal Organization, Inc. (VALOR)*, www.valor-national.org, a nonprofit organization, was established in 1979 by the late Frank G. Carrington, one of the early proponents of victims' rights. It was his intention that the organization provide leadership on issues related to the rights of crime victims in America. Carrington has often been referred to as the "father of the crime victims' rights movement in America," and VALOR has consistently pursued the vision that was his trademark.

+ *Mothers Against Drunk Drivers (MADD)*, www.madd.org, is an organization of mothers and other family members dedicated to helping those who have lost loved ones to the violence of drunk drivers. They offer advocacy, victims services, and educational programs for survivors. They have raised awareness of drunk driving and sought stricter law enforcement. If you have lost someone because of a drunk driver, MADD can assist in finding resources that will help you.

+ *National Center for Victims of Crime (NCVC)*, www.ncvc.org, is a national organization founded in 1985, dedicated to serving individuals, families, and communities harmed by crime. They offer help for victims and survivors to find resources and referrals, work to change public policy to help crime victims, and offer training for individuals and agencies involved in victims' rights. They have a hotline to serve victims and survivors of violent crime: 1-800-394-2255.

Therapies

A NOTE ABOUT POST-TRAUMATIC STRESS DISORDER (PTSD)

Before we can begin any discussion of therapies, we need to consider the possibility that in the aftermath of losing a loved one to violence, some survivors will develop post-traumatic stress disorder (PTSD).

According the *Diagnostic and Statistical Manual of Mental Disorders*, such a person has been exposed to an extreme traumatic stressor in which *both* of the following were present:

1. The person directly experienced an event or events that involved actual threat or serious injury or other threat to one's physical integrity; or the person witnessed an event or events that involved death, injury or a threat to the physical integrity of a person or the person learned about unexpected or violent death, serious harm, or threatening injury experienced by a family member or to other close associates, and,
2. The person's response to the event or event must involve intense fear, helplessness, or horror.

The following symptoms must be present for a diagnosis of PTSD:

+ Recurrent and intrusive distressing recollections or dreams about the event
+ Feeling as if the traumatic event were recurring, such as through hallucinations and flashbacks which last from a few seconds to a number of hours
+ Intense psychological distress at cues that symbolize the event
+ Physiological reactivity upon exposure to internal or external cues (triggers) which resemble an aspect of the traumatic event. (e.g., a woman who was raped in an elevator breaks out in a sweat when entering any elevator)

Additionally, these symptoms must endure for more than a month and must cause clinically significant distress or functional impairment.

Obviously, as a survivor, you will experience distress at what happened to you and your loved one. However, it is the level of distress, the number of symptoms, how severe they are, and how they affect your life that will decide whether you have a clinical diagnosis of PTSD. For example, both Keisha and Louise had symptoms of PTSD, but Keisha was "clinically diagnosed," whereas Louise was not:

Louise's husband ran a convenience store. He was shot to death in a burglary. Although Louise did not witness the murder, she experienced the following symptoms: overwhelming grief, nightmares about the robbery, sleeplessness, and depression. Louise imagined distressing images of what had happened; however, she did not experience intrusive flashbacks or hallucinations about the actual event. She was able to function (that is, get out of bed, eat, and communicate). Her grief of course, was overwhelming, but the level of distress in her life was manageable. She also had an excellent support system. So, while Louise had some symptoms of PTSD, she did not meet the criteria for a clinical diagnosis.

On the other hand, Keisha's flashbacks of her rape and her boyfriend's murder were based in her own reality of the events. She found herself paralyzed by fear and unable to go out. She experienced nightmares, sleeplessness, and intrusive memories of the trauma. These symptoms collectively impaired the way she functioned, and persisted for more than one month. Keisha needed intensive treatment to learn how to handle the flashbacks, fear, and anxiety. Gradually, over time, she was able to reconstruct her life. It was a long and painful process, one that still haunts her today.

I believe that many who lose someone through violence, especially those who have either witnessed or been part of it, will experience some degree of PTSD, even without a clinical diagnosis. A 1990 study on the impact of homicide on surviving family members indicated that, regardless of the specific character of the crime, 23.4 percent develop PTSD after the death of their loved one. Researchers recommend all homicide survivors be screened for the presence of PTSD and be provided with counseling referrals.

Not everyone will develop PTSD. If the trauma is dealt with quickly, the severity of reactions may be eased and the risk of developing PTSD is diminished. A therapist can help you determine how severe your symptoms are and what steps to take for its treatment. He or she can help you to restructure the fragments of your life and to accept that there may be some irrevocable changes brought about by the trauma. The process used in treating PTSD is usually a combination of psychotherapy and medication, which safely reintroduces you to the trauma and gives you tools to rebuild, much as this book does. In fact, if you suspect you have PTSD, do use this book in conjunction with your therapy.

You may find that you need professional help during your journey, whether you suffer from PTSD or not. There are many types of therapies available and in the following pages you will find them divided into these areas:

+ Psychological
+ Hypnotherapy
+ Group therapy
+ Medical
+ holistic mind/body
+ Spiritual
+ Art
+ Nature

These are not mutually exclusive; in fact, used in combination, these therapies can offer comprehensive benefits to your health. For example, you may choose to see your medical doctor, attend therapy, speak to your clergy person, and also begin a good exercise program. Please take advantage of as many resources as you can.

PSYCHOLOGICAL

Many forms of therapy are available today. Individual therapy is the choice of many people. In individual therapy, you will have the opportunity to privately share your story with and then be guided by a skilled therapist through the unfolding feelings and experiences of your trauma. When Claire's husband, Jim, was murdered, she realized she needed to talk to someone:

> Jim was my rock. We were married for so long; I always confided in him and felt protected. When he was murdered, I felt naked, alone, terrified. I never considered counseling before, but I needed someone to talk to. I needed someone who was objective and would listen to my fears. In some ways, I needed someone to be like Jim was, to listen to me and help me until I could do it myself. I needed someone to show me the way. Therapy helped; I was glad I did it.

Individual therapy has the advantage of providing complete confidentiality between you and your therapist, as well as his or her full attention for the session. As for what kind of therapist to consult, you have a choice of several. A psychiatrist, for example, is a medical doctor with a specialty in psychiatry, and is the only mental health professional who can prescribe drugs. A psychologist, on the other hand, has a PhD in psychology, can have many varied trainings, but cannot write prescriptions.

There are also therapists and counselors who may have training in psychology without actually having a medical or doctoral degree: A psychotherapist has a graduate degree or MA in psychology or related fields, and can, like the psychologist, have many different specialties and training. Social workers, or MSWs, have graduate degrees and, depending on their training, can offer various kinds of therapy.

All of these professionals can offer you counseling. However, not everyone has specific experience in or training for grief counseling, particularly as it may relate to violence.

A word of caution here: because of the extreme trauma and special circumstances associated with violence, some professionals are uncomfortable dealing with such an event and the suffering its survivors experience. Therefore, there can be a tendency to overmedicate rather than talk through the problem. While antidepressants can be useful, many other drugs such as tranquilizers can actually work against you in the long run. The hard work of suffering has to be done. Drugs might make it easier, but you cannot avoid it. If you try to cover the effects with medication, you may develop a dependency and actually weaken yourself, rather than gathering the real strength you need for your journey. Before you take any medication, talk to your therapist or medical doctor about the potential for dependency. Remember that while something to help in the beginning when the trauma is the most extreme may be beneficial, sooner or later you will have to face what you and I know is true—someone has taken our loved one away, and nothing will ever change that. You have a choice about how you will face that truth, so remember, using drugs will only work temporarily—and delay the inevitable—facing and learning to live with the truth.

Even if the person comes highly recommended, or you may have consulted him or her before for other matters, you are within your rights to select a therapist who can provide the special kind of counseling needed in the aftermath of a violent act. When I was in practice in Colorado, prior to Aaron's death, a woman named Nan came to see me after her daughter, Julie, had been murdered. Nan was grieving and needed help. I saw her for over a year. I remember thinking, "Good God, how can I help this woman who has experienced such an awful trauma?" I sat with her while she cried; I empathized, had compassion, and used the techniques I had learned to counsel her. I tried to help, but I knew that I couldn't possibly understand her experience and wondered what I could do to help her. I was aware that the means and tools I had, while good, were inadequate. At that time, I had no model that addressed the effects of violent crime in a truly meaningful way, one that specifically addressed the needs of families and friends of murder victims. This was before Columbine, 9/11, and other violent events had raised awareness in the mental health community of the need for grief counseling. Nationally, we were still in a state of denial, and I was unaware of the stigma that survivors faced and of what course of action to take. I listened, used Elisabeth Kübler-Ross's classic stages of grief, and was as empathetic as I could be. After Aaron's death, I realized the depth I had been missing during my counseling of Nan. With Nan, I was on the outside looking in, using tools and a clumsy model that actually separated us rather than bringing us together. This created a distance between her and me, as if there were a glass barrier between us—one through which I could see her but not join her. One in which I could safely stay on the outside. Now, the glass has been shattered; now, when I speak with victims of violence, I do understand what they are going through, I am right there with them. I often think of Nan and how I could have helped her, knowing what I know now.

When a violent crime affected me, I was instantly and acutely aware of the limitations of regular therapeutic models. In fact, that was one of the reasons I stayed out of therapy until I learned about Families of Murder Victims. You, too, might find yourself avoiding therapy because you know instinctively that, while people might "understand," they really don't know how you feel and you don't want to take the risk of sharing your story with someone who will not really hear it correctly.

It may be difficult for you to open up to a complete stranger about what happened. You want to be left alone, in a safe environment. While I understand these feelings and did that for a while myself, I also realized that my isolation was taking me further out of the world I needed to live in. I needed to tell my story to and get help from someone I could trust.

What you need to do is find someone who has experience with extreme trauma and violent crime. This takes special, professional skills, not just the person's personal experience with violence. In support groups, you will find help from people who have experienced similar trauma and this is invaluable; however, a therapist is different, he or she should have professional counseling skills. Beware of *ad hoc* counselors, without medical or psychology credentials, who may not yet have resolved their own crises; they are not in a position to counsel you professionally.

When you decide to consult a therapist, ask people you know, including your health practitioners, if they can recommend a professional therapist whom they trust *and* who has experience working with violence. If they don't, try the resources in the appendix and also consult the list of victims services organizations I have included here.

Please keep in mind that it will be important for you to feel a connection with your therapist. Ask yourself the following questions:

+ Can I open myself to this person?
+ Do I feel comfortable?
+ What are his/her credentials and training? (Feel free to questions the therapist. Ask outright about his/her training and perspective on violent crime.)
+ How can he/she help me?

Marianne, whose daughter, Vicki, was murdered by her boyfriend said,

> It was really important for me to relate to my therapist. I didn't want to go to someone I felt uncomfortable with or couldn't talk to. I want to feel that this person is on my side and understands me because I want to tell him or her things I don't tell anyone. I also wanted someone who had some experience dealing with violence. I knew that my story was shocking, I also knew that most people couldn't handle it. I interviewed two different therapists before I found someone I felt I could trust and would be able to open up to.

A caveat here, while some therapists may not have training in trauma counseling, many can and will do a good job helping you—if you cannot find anyone with specific trauma skills, then question the therapist you may have been referred to and find out what their approach and treatment will be and then decide whether you can make a connection with this person.

Remember that the therapeutic relationship is in many ways the most revealing and intimate one you will have, therefore it is important you pick someone you feel you can freely express yourself to and with whom you can develop trust.

HYPNOTHERAPY

Hypnotherapy is a valuable approach to therapy. It is not, as some stage acts would like us to believe, a technique whereby people will cluck like chickens!

Hypnosis has been shown to be effective in treating grief, flashbacks, anxiety, pain management, habit changes, and sports performance. It is a powerful therapy in which the client, through a series of suggestions and cues, enters a relaxed but focused state of attention (not a state of unconsciousness). In this focused state, he or she can recover and utilize inner strengths and resources that may be repressed or forgotten and use them for the intense work of grief and suffering.

GROUP THERAPY

In this kind of therapy, you will be in a group setting, sharing your experiences with others. A trained therapist leads and facilitates, helping everyone in the group. The group leader may have a topic for the evening or use another format to encourage all members to speak. The advantage of group therapy is that you will meet others who are experiencing something similar to you so, of course, you will want to look for a group that most closely identifies with your trauma. When Lisa's mother, Marie, was killed in a vehicular homicide, Lisa found out about an appropriate support group:

> Going to the support group was hard at first, I felt like we were victims, stigmatized because we were in a group where everyone had lost someone to violence. But I learned that that was part of the problem. I did feel different, alone. But sitting there with everyone else made me feel less isolated and I could learn how other people dealt with what I was going through. I met a woman whose background was similar to mine, we became friends during the group and it was wonderful to have her to talk to.

Many friendships form during attendance of support groups. Relationships that began in sharing sorrow and loss can become strong bonds for future happiness, as each of you moves forward. It is like having a companion on a journey you thought you would have to take alone.

MEDICAL

The stress that occurs during and after losing someone to violence can have serious health consequences. You may also have been involved in the violence directly, in some way that affected you physically, such as in the case of Keisha; or perhaps your shock or other emotional state is now causing your body to react in unhealthy ways. In any case, if you are not feeling physically well or "like yourself," it is important to consult the medical community for assistance.

Often, survivors will not eat, or they overeat. Some will forget about their health entirely and smoke, drink, or take drugs. You may feel aches and pains, real and imaginary. Even if your body is fine, you may imagine that you really have something wrong with you, when in fact it is the stress that makes you feel this way. This might take the form of heart palpitations, breathlessness, faintness or dizziness, fatigue, or weakness. Your limbs may feel too heavy to move.

After Aaron's death, I was exhausted and felt weak most of the time. I experienced aches and pains I'd never had before. During moments of intense grief, I would feel as though I were having a heart attack—I felt like my heart was being destroyed, which certainly, emotionally, it was. I began to think I was suffering from all kinds of ailments. it was frightening. I went to my doctor, who reassured me that my heart, at least physically, was fine. I had, however, lost twenty pounds, and had no desire for food. After a blood test, it was discovered I was anemic. At first, I didn't care. Looking back, I realize how battered I was and how I just seemed to float along, not really caring much about my health. When I realized that my anemia was getting worse, I started eating better. It was a wake-up call that if I didn't take care of myself, it was going to make my journey that much harder.

Remember that while there is no cure for grief, punishing yourself physically and emotionally is not the answer. You can make it easier on yourself and those you love by taking steps to care for yourself. Do consider having a thorough checkup, telling your doctor what happened, and what your symptoms are, however trivial or unrelated they may seem, so that he/she can rule out any serious medical issues and help you recognize which symptoms may be the physical effects of the trauma.

HOLISTIC MIND/BODY

Holistic, or alternative, therapies are valuable methods of treatment and can help you heal from a more "whole" perspective. During my graduate training, I studied somatics, which comes from the Greek word *sōma*, meaning body. The principle is that we have a bodily experience of the trauma, and that to ignore it is to neglect a truly important part of our whole person.

Violence will change your body as well as your mind. Your body tells your story. It needs to be heard and helped. There are many somatic modalities to choose from, all of which are treatments that use touch as part of the therapy. For example, the Rosen evolved out of physical therapy. Marion Rosen, the founder of this modality, found that while she was working on a patient's tight muscles or a painful part of the body, if she applied gentle touch and asked the person what was being felt, the person would often remember what had happened when the pain first occurred. She discovered that people's bodies will often hold a "memory" of an experience and that by gently applying touch at that tensed part of the body while a person speaks about that memory, the muscle could soften its contraction and often the person would experience relief.

While these are not specific treatments for trauma, they may be beneficial in conjunction with other therapies and may help you deal with the effects of trauma on your body.

I use the overarching principle of somatics in my work: our bodies are a vital, living part of our experience. We are not separate, discrete parts—mind, body, and spirit—but integrated, whole human beings, and our approach to treatment and health should reflect this. Please check the resources in the appendix for more information about somatics if this form of therapy sounds like something you'd like to try.

In addition to somatics, there are many other holistic therapies to choose from. The following is a list of treatments for you to consider:

+ *Chinese medicine, or acupuncture,* is a system whereby tiny needles are inserted along the meridians, which are points of energy in the body that support the organs. Different combinations of points are used for different ailments. Acupuncture is a valuable asset to our Western approaches to medicine and therapy. It can help balance your body, lower blood pressure, and relieve many types of pain.
+ *Chiropractic services* are well known for back care and adjustments of spine and neck. Many chiropractic services include nutritional support and wellness services, and can help you form an overall plan for your health.
+ *Nutritional support* is important during and after trauma. When we are stressed, we may suffer deficiencies in our diet

because of either not eating or overeating. Valerie's struggle is
a common one:

> I always had issues with my weight. I ate when I was
> stressed or depressed. When Devon was murdered, I
> started eating to stop the pain. I gained weight, which
> made my lower-back pain worse. I went to a chiroprac-
> tor who helped my back, and I saw a nutritionist who
> helped me get on a good eating plan. It took a while,
> but I started to get some control over what I was eat-
> ing and my weight, which in turn made me feel better
> about my life.

You will want to look at your own nutritional needs and find
out what you may need to maintain your body, so that the very
real dangers of deficiencies do not make an already traumatic
situation worse.

+ *Massage* is a wonderful way to take care of yourself. A good
massage by a licensed therapist will help the toxins caused by
stress to move out of your body. It will relax and nourish you,
and may help you to sleep better. It really helped Lisa following
her mother's death:

> I knew I had to de-stress somehow. My body was so
> worn out from the days in the hospital before mom
> died. I was working full time and trying to take care
> of my own family. Massage was something for me. It
> soothed and nurtured me. My neck wasn't so tight all
> the time. It was well worth the relief for me.

There are many different forms of massage to choose from.
Swedish is the most common, which is a system long strokes of
various levels of pressure to address tensions all over the body.
Other types of massage include aromatherapy, which uses
beneficial aromas in the therapy; Thai; and shiatsu.

✦ **Yoga** is a system of body-based postures developed centuries
   ago in India, often as a preparation for meditation. Today, yoga
   is widely available, and taught in studios, gyms, wellness centers, and many other locations; some private yoga instructors
   will even come to your home or office. Yoga will help you keep
   flexible, and develop strength, calmness, and a sense of peace.
   There are many forms of yoga, from Hatha, which is commonly
   practiced, to the new "hot," or Bikram, yoga, which involves
   doing the postures in a room whose thermostat has been set to
   a high temperature—not for the faint-hearted! If you are just
   beginning, talk to the yoga teacher at your location and ask her
   what would be good for your circumstances. You may find that
   this ancient discipline is an excellent way for you to de-stress.

✦ **Dance and movement therapies** use specific movements and
   dance techniques to help you move through the feelings you are
   experiencing. It is a powerful way for you to use your body as
   a forum for expression, and has helped many people to move
   through painful memories and traumas. Movement and dance
   can be used informally as well. All cultures use dance as a way
   of expressing joy, sorrow, and celebration. Certainly, after your
   trauma, you will not feel like dancing, but perhaps that is the
   time you most need to try it.

   If you like to dance and can manage it, put on a favorite
   piece of music and see where your legs will take you. Sometimes
   by dancing, you can manage to have a reprieve from the daily
   sadness you find yourself living in. For that moment, you can
   move and feel alive—and for that you will feel grateful.

   Movement is itself a powerful exercise. Even if you cannot
   dance due to actual physical constraints; you can move those
   parts of your body that you are able to, even if it is the smallest
   movement.

✦ **Physical exercise** is vitally important in your struggle after
   trauma. If you are able to exercise and can get to a gym, very
   good. If this is new to you, ask a trainer or read an exercise
   manual to help you with a program appropriate for you. Ease

into a program by trying ten minutes a day at a gym or try walking instead of taking the bus. Or park farther away than you normally would, to give yourself a chance to exercise. Indeed, if you are able to take a walk, then by all means, do. The simple act of walking can be a healing therapy, changing your view and letting you take a fresh, new breath.

If you already exercise, then you know its value. It's even more important now to help you gain or keep your strength. Make a commitment to start again, today, even if it's only for ten minutes. Then increase it until you are back to pretrauma levels, although, it is fair to say that you may never get back completely, for a long time—and you need to accept that and do what you can.

The therapies above all have one thing in common: they address the importance of the body in your overall well-being. They are very useful in conjunction with psychotherapy and support groups; they ensure that you are allowing your body to be part of the healing process. In my own practice, I encourage people to include some form of physical activity in addition to psychological therapy. I find that it is much more helpful than simply addressing the mental and emotional trauma we experience. However, I do realize that when you are in the beginning of your journey, you will probably not be able to do many of these things. It may be all you can do just to be able to withstand the shock and overwhelming feelings you are experiencing. This is normal; these are only health suggestions for you to use as you feel appropriate.

SPIRITUAL

In chapter 2, you learned that the value of religion and spirituality was one of the eight life preservers to hold on to in your journey. Now, we are concerned with what resources may relate to your faith and spiritual practices. For example, if you are a member of a religious or spiritual congregation, you may wish to talk to your clergyperson about what has happened. He or she may be able to offer you counseling and comfort during these times. Many religious and spiritual services are themselves designed to help a person through the terrible pain and effects of a traumatic event. The funeral or memorial service is a ritual designed to provide comfort and closure for you and your family and, although, I am sure you will be in shock while it is going on, it could bring some peace to you.

Ron, about whom you read earlier, tells how a spiritual ritual helped him:

> After Debra was murdered, I was lost. My rabbi suggested I say the Kaddish, the prayer we say for [a] lost loved one every day for a year. I did that for Debra. It helped me go through many levels of my loss for her. It changed, too, through the year. At first there was no peace; I was angry and full of guilt. Later, I would notice that, after the prayer, I could talk to my rabbi without anger. I looked forward to that time of prayer every day. It was a way to ease the terrible emptiness I felt and I was grateful for it.

Religious rituals and services are meant to help us during the most profound times of our lives—birth, marriage, sickness, death, and grief. They offer solace and hope for those of us who suffer. We come together as a community to gain support and strength.

At Aaron's funeral mass, many of his friends from Franciscan were present, and they performed the music for the mass. His friend, Chris Ledyard, sang this song, which gave me hope that I would see Aaron again:

> Oh, brother of mine
> We'll see you on the other side
> Oh, dear friend of mine,
> We'll see you on the other side
> Oh, sweet child of mine
> I'll see you on the other side

Hearing this music was a great comfort to me—and while I was hardly able to stand up during the funeral, it helped me to see how many people loved and honored Aaron is his life and wanted to be there for him now.

Besides or instead of embracing formal spiritual traditions, you may want to try spiritual healing, which is offered through a variety of practitioners. There are many gifted healers and spiritual directors, who may be found through such organizations as Healing Touch or The International Center for Reiki Training, or by speaking with a spiritual director.

Many cultures have distinct spiritual healing practices; for example, Native American, African, Brazilian, or other communities use special rituals and observances to honor the passing of a loved one. A Native American sage said the following:

> Death is not the end, it is only a change from one world to another. If you love life, death will not be so frightening, but a time to celebrate one's passage from one existence to another. When you leave this world, open your mind and leave with a prayer in your heart—realize that where there is love, fear cannot live. When someone you love leaves this world, even in violence, realize that the soul of this person is free to soar to the Great Spirit, our common Creator.

The Tibetan Book of Living and Dying, a powerful, eloquent book by Sogyal Rinpoche, helps us help us understand Buddhist rituals, spiritual practices, and principles, to help us honor both how we live and how we face death. This following is a passage from the book:

> Pray you will survive and discover the richest possible meaning to the new life you now find yourself in. Be vulnerable and receptive, be courageous, and be patient.

Above all, look into your life to find ways of sharing
your love more deeply with others now.

We are collectively drawn together by our human experience of
living and dying, and have developed rich treasure to help us through
our loss and sorrow. Keep your heart open to hear what spiritual
leaders have to say and allow their wisdom to guide you.

PRAYER AND MEDITATION

Two resources that I believe can profoundly impact your experience
are prayer and meditation. Prayer is religious as well as spiritual,
whereas meditation can be religious, spiritual, or secular. There are
many, many types of prayer and ways to pray. Many of us are familiar with the kind of prayer that asks God to give us something. We
pray for ourselves or someone we know. We ask for specific favors
or the answers to a problem. Diane said the following about prayer:

> I didn't really think much about prayer, except maybe
> to get me out of a pinch or help me win something! I
> used to make deals with God in my prayer: I'll do this,
> if you give me that. Then after my parents were killed,
> I was so overwhelmed, I just prayed for help—any help.
> I felt that it did help me, because I didn't feel so alone,
> it gave me something to hold on to.

Prayer may not be something you can do or want to do. You may
not believe in prayer or may have lost what faith you did have. This
is a normal response to such violent events: you are shocked, angry,
hurt, and lash out any notion of a god who could have allowed such
a horrible thing to happen—as Michael felt:

> I don't pray, I never have. I don't believe in it—does
> that make me a bad person? After my daughter Laura

> was murdered, I still did not change my beliefs. People
> kept telling me I should pray and believe, and made it
> sound like there was something wrong with me. This
> added more hurtful feelings to an already devastating
> experience. I wish people would think about what they
> are saying and remember not everyone believes what
> they do.

Michael has a very good point. People should be given the respect to grieve in each their own way. If you wish, you can pray for them, but please, do not force your views on someone else. If you are a person who never prayed or believed in prayer, or once did but cannot bring yourself to pray, you are entitled to think and feel the way you do. Don't allow yourself to feel pressured into behaving hypocritically, to feign spiritual behaviors you do not actually feel. Your emotions and how you handle them are your own business.

If you do wish to pray, there are many beautiful prayers available in all religious and spiritual traditions in the world. Try to remember a prayer that was special to you or your family. Maybe today, all you will be able to do is ask for the willingness to pray— and that will have to be good enough.

Meditation is a technique of focused attention. Many of our world religions practice meditation in one form or another. Buddhists, in particular, have a rich history of meditation, and there are many excellent guidelines available for developing a daily practice. In all faiths throughout the world, meditation has been used to deepen the connection to the divine. From a secular standpoint, meditation has been shown to be an effective resource for stress management, better health, and better concentration.

I began meditating in 1982. Through the years, I have tried many different approaches to both prayer and meditation. I have studied different systems and have developed a method that I call Modern Meditation. Over the years, I had relied on daily prayer and this kind of meditation, and they shored up my strength and faith. This experience helped me immensely when Aaron died. Then, despite my devastation and absolute horror and grief, I could still call upon my morning meditation and prayer to gain the strength and comfort I desperately needed.

My method is a simple, three-step secular approach that is easy to learn. The three steps are:

1. Relax the body.
2. Calm the mind.
3. Free the spirit.

If you are interested in learning Modern Meditation, you can get more information in the appendix or go directly to my Web site, www.kathleenohara.com.

There are many other forms of meditation that you can choose from. Many wellness centers and gyms offer meditation classes; also, there is a host of different CDs you can order to learn methods ranging from the simple to the advanced. Whichever method you choose, I hope you take the time to keep with it and develop something that has helped so many. It is a gift you will give yourself that will serve you again and again.

ART

Art is among the greatest of gifts we possess as human beings. It is a powerful resource for us to use at any time. It can lift our spirits, make us cry, and give us inspiration to live. There are many forms of art, including painting, sculpture, drawing, and photography, as well as music and literature. Any or all of these may inspire, heal and help you.

Incorporate art into your life. This can be as simple as going to a museum; looking at the paintings, sculptures, and drawings; and allowing them to lift you into another world. Or you could listen to your favorite piece or music (or find a new one). Or, go to a bookstore or library and find a book that speaks to and encourages you.

Art is a wonderful therapeutic tool. An art therapist can help you express your feelings through an artistic medium. He or she will ask you to draw or paint certain feelings you have. (By the way, this doesn't mean you have to be an "artist"; it simply means you use a visual medium to express yourself.) The therapist will encourage you to work through feelings by expressing them in your art. Many children are helped through grief by art therapy, as their language capabilities may not yet be sufficiently developed for them to express themselves verbally.

Music is another excellent resource for you to use. Much of our world's music echoes our human experience of joy, sorrow, inspiration, and love. Try putting on a favorite piece of music and allow it to take it where it will. It may be painful to hear music that held particular meaning for you and your loved one, but may prove a powerful catharsis if you are able to wring every drop of feeling out of it as you listen and recall your being together or your mutual pleasure in such compositions. It's your choice: you can allow music to help you grieve, or to uplift you. Music that wails will do some of your crying for you; music that is beautiful will give you hope and pleasure, in even your darkest moments. Use it to enhance or change your mood, as you see fit.

We will discuss art in much more detail when we come to stage 6. There, you will be asked to create—but here, I am more concerned with your using art as an existing resource to draw upon. However, if you want to use creativity more actively now, than jump right into stage 6 and start creating.

NATURE

Sometimes nature is the most healing of all the resources we have available to us. Nature shows us the cycles of life and death from the gentle but wild birth of spring to the inevitable death of winter, only to begin again the following spring. The beauty of nature is that it is always changing, moving through each of the seasons—as are our lives.

Many of us can see the ones we love in the sunrise, the vast ocean, or the sweetness of a flower. Nature gives us her comfort freely; we only have to look and see. You can find her wherever you are, whether it is out your window or in a garden, in a forest, or along a shore. Even the densest metropolis has trees, flowers, parks, birds, and sky. Take some time to take a fresh look and let the power of nature bring healing to you. Visit a zoo or animal sanctuary, and rejoice in the innumerable forms of life that our Earth supports. If you live in the mountains, near the oceans, or on the plains, there is, I am sure, a lovely landscape to look at or stroll along. Even if you live in an urban setting, go on a hike, whatever the season, and enjoy the exercise and the view. If you aren't near a park, walk through a residential area that has gardens. Once, when I was feeling particularly parched for nature, and was in the city in the dead of winter, I went into a flower shop and looked at all the flowers and took in the colors and smells, just to be reminded of something alive—I did buy some, since I was just standing around smelling all of them!

The point is that nature, in all its myriad forms, ever offers us her beauty and a healing balm for your pain.

The Choice Is Yours

NOW, YOU HAVE told your story and shaped it into the burden you carry. You have found eight life preservers within yourself, to strengthen you. Now, you are choosing among all the available external resources the ones you may want to use to as your lighthouses in the harbor, there to guide you when the waves of grief come fast and hard, and the darkness threatens to close in on you. You are not alone; they are there for you as you move forward in your journey.

Stage 4

The Ocean of Grief

LEARNING TO RIDE THE WAVES

You have been grieving since the moment your story began. Stage 4 will teach you how to ride the waves that come out of the oceans of grief. No matter where you are in your journey, this chapter will offer many good suggestions to help you manage these powerful feelings, especially during the first year.

If you have never before experienced the death of someone close to you, whether or not it involved violence, you may need to learn how to grieve because you are unprepared for its intensity, for its lasting power. Others who do not know the weight of such feelings may think you are overreacting or malingering, and tell you to "get over it" or "move on." Unless someone has been there, they just don't know the depth of that ocean. And you, yourself, may feel impatient to heal, and angry with yourself because it isn't happening more quickly. It will take as long as it takes . . . alas, nobody can simply will it to end.

Beth, who lost her son in the Iraq war told me the following:

It's been only six months since Nicholas was killed in
Iraq and everyone, including the counselors, just want
us to be okay. But we aren't—we are not okay, we can't
just "move on."

This grief of yours is not something that can be neatly packaged
into a predictable measure of time. Grief is a powerful process that
affects each person differently. You cannot get over it just so others
can feel comfortable. Grief is often unrelenting, disruptive, and ever-
present, but *it will get better*. But not before we have done the hard
work of overcoming it by learning to ride its tumultuous waves.

The concept of waves may sound like a cliché, but that is how
many experience grief—we are hit by tidal waves of emotions,
which seemingly come out of nowhere. But they don't come out of
nowhere—they erupt from an unchecked volcano teeming with many
different powerful feelings associated with our loss, such as:

+ Extreme sorrow and pain
+ Confusion
+ Guilt
+ "Crazy" feelings
+ Loneliness
+ Fear
+ Anger

Extreme Sorrow and Pain

AFTER AARON'S FUNERAL, everyone went home. The house
was quiet. And that's when it started in earnest: grief came hard,
often, and relentlessly. I felt intense, visceral pain any time of day
or night—always unexpectedly, unpredictably. Sometimes it felt
like a hammer was beating me on the head, or a baseball bat was
hitting my body. Emotions rushed at me; I called this assault "the
torturers," because I needed to have a way of shaping my grief into

something I could begin to manage. Just as I had to shape my story into something that would not crush me, I had to do the same for my grief, because in its raw form it threatened to destroy me. When my emotions battered me, I finally would give in, feeling the pain, begging them to leave. The remarkable thing was that, as I allowed the torturers to find me, I discovered that these feelings wouldn't destroy me. And so, I allowed grief to do its work. Not because I wanted to but because I had to. The torture was coming from within, and it was my job to let it out.

Many people I have met personally and professionally talk about the intensity of grief. We are fearful we will not be able to survive our emotions; we believe they will destroy us. Rita shared this with me:

> After my Don, my companion of twenty years, was shot and killed; I felt overwhelming waves of grief. I didn't know how to handle them. I was afraid that they would drown me. I had never experienced anything this strong. I realized I knew nothing about grief. I became frightened of it—I tried to avoid it, but there was no escape. The waves just kept coming, at any time or place. I learned to let them come; I would cry and scream and let it out, and then they would go. They didn't destroy me; if anything, I learned that I was stronger than I thought.

Many of us are like Rita; we don't think we can withstand this pain. It is something we are never prepared for, even if grief has touched us before. When these waves come, try to realize that they are just that—huge waves of emotion *that will pass*, if you let them. If it helps, give your grief a name; perhaps you will call it "the torturers," as I did, or something else that has meaning to you. Rita called them "Hurricane R," which helped her to gain control over them. She learned how to ride out the hurricane and knew that it wouldn't destroy her; it was her grief and she had to let it pass through and over her before it would leave.

The principle here is to be able to withstand the assault of grief—and realize that while it is a powerful force, you are stronger than and will survive it. There is no easy way around these feelings. You must accept that you are dealing with the natural forces of grief—strong, powerful, and often overwhelming—but they will pass. If you were standing on the beach and a huge wave came, you might try to run, but that wouldn't help. You might try to fight it, but that wouldn't work either. Fighting it will only dig you in deeper. Ultimately, it is better to recognize, to put a name to your grief, rather than denying its existence or power, and learn to ride it out.

When a wave approaches, take a deep breath and use your life preservers, any or all of the eight qualities: courage, hope, faith or spirituality, optimism, humor, patience, joy, and compassion. Say the following: "I have _____ (fill in the quality). I will ride _____ (fill in the name you have given them). These waves will not destroy me, they are part of my grief. I will survive."

After the waves come, rest. You will be exhausted—this is a time for sleeping and regenerating. This grief will take time to pass over and subside; there are no hard and fast rules, but I can tell you from my own experience and others' that it will grow softer, with more time between waves.

After losing her ten-year-old son, Linda said,

> I could barely cope with the constant grief, especially the first six months. It seemed like I would just get up from one wave, and another would come. I didn't think they would ever stop. I learned to breathe, and ride, and then one day, I realized they were still coming, but it had changed—they were a little easier for me.

A note of caution here: do not put an expiration time on your grief. Everyone will feel it at his or her own pace. Many report that the first year is the most emotionally battering—while this may be true, no one can tell you what is the "right" way to grieve. Remember that inner resource of patience? Now is the time to apply it to yourself. Be patient with your feelings. Listen to them, instead of running away. Let them say their piece and they will let go of their own accord.

Confusion

FEELINGS OF CONFUSION are common in a time of grief. Life has been turned upside down; shock has thrown you into an alternative reality where things don't make sense. Why would they? Yesterday, your life had certain boundaries and anchors, now you are reeling, unmoored, shaken loose by the violence that swept away your loved one.

Sometimes in our grief, we will have to learn to live all over again, as Mary learned:

> After my daughter Amy committed suicide, I found it hard to relate to the world as it was now. It was so disorienting—things were strange and didn't make sense. It was though I had to learn how to walk and eat and talk all over again. I forgot how to live; I didn't remember life before she died.

You may relate to Mary's experience. Perhaps you feel disoriented; you may have forgotten some of even the most basic of functions. You may have to take special care to remember to eat or take a shower. You may need the help of your family or friends to remind you of and/or assist you in small, mundane tasks and chores.

In addition to confusion, we may experience feelings of denial. For me, summers were more difficult because, during the winter, Aaron was away at school; I wouldn't see him much. I could pretend he was away at school. In the summer, my grief was worse because I expected him to be home. The first summer after his death, I was going into a food store and I saw a young man pushing the shopping carts together. He had a baseball cap on and, from the side, looked like Aaron. For a moment, I thought, "Oh, there he is, thank God, this was all just a big mistake and he's been here all the time!" In the next moment, the boy turned his head; it wasn't Aaron. (You, too, may have already experienced false sightings of a loved one. They may not lessen in number in time, but the surge of false hope and then pangs of disappointment will lessen eventually when they do occur.)

 FAMILY AND FRIENDS can help a grieving person who has begun neglecting him or herself by asking simple questions like: "Did you eat today?" or better yet, "I am bringing some food over, we'll eat together." Ask if he or she would like your company for the night, if insomnia is a problem; your presence may enable the person to relax and sleep. If you notice that his/her home or body is less kempt than usual, offer to do a load of laundry or to hire in a cleaning service; set out a change of clothing; or present a gift of bath oils and a fluffy towel, and insist the person indulge him/herself while you remain to talk to, there or from another room. Make an appointment, arranging to foot the bill, for the person to visit a hairdresser or a local spa. He or she may truly be unaware—and may then feel ashamed—that everyday matters like these have slipped so far as to be noticeable to others. Be sensitive when you intervene, as some issues may concern delicate areas of personal dignity.

If you did not witness or had no way of anticipating the death of a loved one, you may feel for some time that the event didn't take place, that there was somehow some mistake of crossed identities, that he or she is going to come strolling in as if never away. These feelings of denial accompany grief because it is so hard to believe what happened is true. You are initially in shock, and the value of that shock is that it protects you from the full reality of your trauma. As the shock wears off, then begins a struggle with both the reality of what happened and the intense desire that it didn't. Yet there is value, too, in this duality; it will help you to grow accustomed to what happened more gradually than having to accept it all at once.

Crazy Feelings

MANY, DURING THEIR grief, feel they have "crazy" feelings and thoughts. We do "crazy" things and even wonder if we have lost our minds. This is something not often spoken about in our culture, yet it is a natural, strong part of grief. In fact, denying it only makes it worse. We are told that we need to "handle" our feelings appropriately, to get control or get over them. People do not appreciate open displays of grief because, frankly, they *are* frightening. Many people simply do not want to witness someone crying inconsolably or otherwise engaging in "the madness of grief." But for survivors of violence, that very madness often lies in the bare facts of our stories, what our loved ones endured. What may have happened to them was literally unthinkable, unspeakable . . . and so are our reactions, and rightly so.

I am reminded of the following occasion: It was the first autumn after Aaron's murder and, when the first cold rain came, I was unprepared for my reaction. I was lying in bed, listening to the rain, when I was gripped by horror. It must be so cold and wet in the ground—maybe the rain would get into Aaron's coffin! He had suffered so much, he couldn't suffer again. I wanted to run to the cemetery and see if the rain was coming in. I worried about what would happen to him. What should I do? I got dressed, ready to go, in a panic that I wouldn't get there in time. Then I wondered how I would know if the rain was getting in. I began to think I was losing my mind. I paced back and forth, thinking about what I could do. I should bring a shovel, but how would I open the coffin?

I know it didn't make sense, but then why would it? The thoughts we think and the sorrows we feel during grief are not entirely rational. I only knew that my child was outside in the rain and I wanted to comfort and protect him, yet I also knew there was nothing I could do to change what had happened to him.

Shakespeare tells us about the madness of grief in *King John*, in which the Lady Constance rants, when she has lost her son,

I am not mad: this hair I tear is mine.
Young Arthur is my son and he is lost
I am not mad; I would to God I were
For then 'tis like I should forget myself
O, if I could, what grief should I forget!
I am not mad; too well, too well I feel
The different plague of each calamity.

When grief makes us feel as if we are going mad, we may do things that surprise us, as Sarah shared with me:

> When I lost my twin sister, I felt literally as though my other half was ripped away from me. Mia was always with me; we shared our world. I felt the physical loss of her. In the beginning, I would talk to her like she was right next to me. I would save a seat for her and buy food for her and tell her jokes. It seemed perfectly normal to me, although I knew when people saw me talking to someone next to me who wasn't really there, they really thought I was losing my mind—but the truth was I didn't lose my mind, I lost my sister.

After Aaron died, his girlfriend, Liz, kept his picture with her everywhere she went. When she went to the movies, she took his picture and put it on the seat next to her, so he could see the movie with her. It took her a long time to finally leave the picture at home.

In your own grief, you may find yourself doing things like these. Have compassion for yourself and recognize that you may need to do these things until you are stronger and can accept your loss more fully. As I've said, and will say again, this is your grief and there is no "right" way to do it. In fact, it is the very personal nature of grief that compels you to experience it in your own way, with your own twists and turns, even your quirks.

Try to apply this exercise to your life, accepting your "madness of grief" as a legitimate emotion. You can write about it, or simply recognize that what you may be doing is your way of making your loss easier for yourself. As "crazy" as you feel, you are having a normal reaction to something that has been catastrophic to you. You are trying to handle enormously powerful feelings—including the fact that the love for the person who is gone has not ceased with that person's heartbeat. It takes time to adjust to so profound and sudden an absence, to be able to let go of the person's presence within your perception of your immediate world. Whenever you wonder if you have lost your mind, remind yourself: you have lost someone you love, not your mind.

Guilt

GUILT IS SURELY one of the most overriding feelings of grief we experience. We torture ourselves with what we could have done differently. We play the scenes of our lives over and over again, and struggle to recall whatever our last conversation was before the tragedy occurred—how casual or trite it may seem now—why couldn't we have expressed our love, said a meaningful good-bye? We judge ourselves harshly, see our faults and magnify them—why weren't we kinder, more generous with our time or attention, and on and on. . . . We make endless lists of what we could have done but didn't do. We beg for just a moment more to love, to change, to make it different, or even for history to rewrite itself, for us to be taken in that person's place. But instead, we are left with the terrible realization that nothing we can do will change what happened and we must learn to live with it. Yet at this point, we cannot—we don't know how.

I talked to Aaron on the phone the day before he was murdered. Earlier that week, I had asked him to come home for Memorial Day. He said he would try to come down in the next few weeks. We chatted for a while, and I was getting ready to go to the store, to get some things to make dinner. I said good-bye and thought nothing more about it.

I agonized over this phone call: Why hadn't I insisted he come home? Why didn't I pay more attention to what he was saying, and why did I allow myself to be distracted by something as insignificant as food shopping? Why, why, why—that word tortured me, ripped me apart, and caused me constant pain. I had to accept that there was nothing I could do now to change one thing that had happened after we spoke—and that was the most devastating thing of all.

Guilt will be a part of your grief, a part you must come to terms with. Guilt is often so intense, it will overwhelm you. It is a natural reaction to hold yourself accountable. But at some point, you will need to realize that guilt is a feeling, not a reality. While it is extraordinarily difficult to break away from guilt, listening to what questions it raises will help you to sort your feelings from the truth. One way to do this is to ask yourself those questions, either in your journal, where you have been writing your story, or even aloud to yourself. Attend to your self-accusations and acknowledge, "Yes, that is what I am feeling," and then ask yourself, "But what is the reality?" Chances are, you already know the answers. You just need to listen to them, too.

Try this exercise:

My guilt "feeling" is (complete the following statements):

I should/shouldn't have . . .
If only I had . . .
Why did I . . . ?
Why didn't I . . . ?
Why did I let _____ happen?

Now change it to this. The reality is:

I did what I thought was best.
I didn't know.
I can't change what happened.
I did the best I could.

You have a choice: you can choose to weigh yourself down with guilt, which will sink you to the bottom, or you can set the weight down and move away. When you become tired of beating yourself up for not controlling everything, stop, take a breath, and let go. It's over, nothing will change that.

Here's another exercise. To exorcise your feelings of guilt, try the following visualization:

> Picture yourself struggling in the ocean to carry this enormous burden—it is so heavy, you feel like you will sink. In this burden are the feelings of guilt over what you did or did not do. Acknowledge that you will have these feelings, but they do not have to crush you. Release the burden—you do not have to carry this—you can let it go. Picture yourself releasing it, watching it sink, and swimming away.

After you complete this exercise, write about it in your journal, or use your support network, talk to your therapist, clergy, friend, or family member, to reinforce the truth that has been released from what has been worrying you.

Loneliness

YOU MAY EXPERIENCE loneliness and isolation. No one can completely feel your innermost sorrow and loss, because it is yours. Nonetheless, you can ask people you care for to journey with you, and know that you are not completely alone. There are hands nearby to guide you, steady you. If you can, reach out to people and talk to them, ask them to be with you. Claire expressed the following about her early days of widowhood:

> I had to find a way to deal with the loneliness I felt after Jim died. It was so hard. I felt like no one could

understand. The truth was they couldn't. But I did talk about it to my friend, Jane. It did help to know someone was there and I wasn't completely alone. She reached out to me and gave me someone to lean on. That didn't make the feeling go away, but I did feel less alone.

Talk about your feelings, let another person know how alone you feel; don't be embarrassed to admit it. I know that no one will banish your inner loneliness; but you do not have to carry it by yourself. That someone can be your best friend, or a mentor who has given you other kinds of guidance, or a therapist. Maybe it is someone who is going through this, too, and understands. This is the value of support groups—you will be with other people who are making the journey, and you can make it together.

 IF YOU KNOW someone who is grieving, you can say something like:

"I know this must be so difficult; if you feel alone, I am here to listen—whatever you want to talk about."

Then really listen to what the person is saying, without interrupting with cheery solutions or commiserating, turning the conversation to how alone you felt during some other experience bearing no relation to this one. *You are simply there to remind the person he or she is not alone.*

Anger

ANGER IS ONE of the most difficult aspects of grief. Many of us are unused to dealing with such strong feelings and may not have good anger management skills. Anger is something we are taught not to show or feel. We often quash or hide it. Often, we don't even know we are angry until it spills out onto someone or something else. But the truth is, in our culture, anger is exploding everywhere. After all, isn't much of our violence fueled by rage and anger, untempered, uncontrolled, and acted out upon someone else?

When someone we love is hurt, we become angry. This is a natural reaction. We want to protect and defend those we love. Therefore, one of the most difficult things to face is that we could not be there to stop the violence, and that we cannot avenge ourselves now that it has occurred. Said Richard:

> I felt anger and guilt that I was not there to stop what happened to Susan. I would have done anything—instead I could do nothing. It happened and I should have been there. I played it over and over in my head; what I would do, how I would change it; I lived in a state of controlled rage, it would spill out when I least expected it and I realized, my anger could kill me or someone else—I had to learn how to deal with it or it would destroy me.

Richard's anger was at himself—he had to come to terms with the fact that he wasn't there, he couldn't protect his wife. He wanted to punish himself for not being there. Richard had to find healthy outlets for his anger so he wouldn't hurt himself or others. He acknowledged that anger is a powerful part of grief, one especially present following violence. The outrage we feel is the outrage we *should* feel. There is no justification for the brutal acts people commit—nor is there an easy remedy for the anger that results from it.

We have to be careful that we do not take our anger out on others, unwittingly or even if we feel there is some justification. We may be reacting on a scale way out of proportion to what is being said or done to us, because we are so wound up and feel we must do *something*. After her rape, Keisha had to learn to deal with her anger. She had been unwittingly taking it out on others, with little or no provocation or reason. She told me the following story:

I was jogging on my usual path in the park. I man was running behind me. My first reaction was terror—Was he chasing me? He got closer, right next to me. I felt anger, which came out of nowhere, and pushed him as he went by. He started; I almost tripped him. He stopped and yelled at me: "Why did you do that?" I turned and ran the other way; thank God he didn't follow me. I knew then I had to deal with this anger before it hurt me or another person.

When Keisha started working with her anger, she had to learn how to express it in ways that would not hurt herself or others. She told her story in therapy; she used a tennis racquet to hit her couch when she felt angry. When she jogged on her usual course, and there were no other people nearby, she spoke her feelings of anger out loud. She took a kickboxing class and empowered herself, kicking her way through her anger. As Keisha learned, there are healthy ways to express and manage anger:

Healthy ways:
+ Creativity, such as writing, painting, sculpting, drawing, music, cooking, sewing, singing, or any form which appeals to you
+ Therapy, either somatic or talk, through support groups or one-on-one
+ Exercise: walking, running, kickboxing, sparring, fencing, martial arts
+ Anger management techniques: punching bags, using a tennis racquet to hit a bed or sofa, going to the woods and yelling, and a variety of other techniques offered in therapy or groups
+ Recognizing where it is coming from and not inflicting it on others
+ Understanding it is a natural part of grief and it will take time to overcome

Unhealthy ways:

+ Taking it out on other innocent people or animals
+ Taking it out on yourself
+ Self-medicating or using addictions to cope (drugs, alcohol, gambling, workaholism, etc.—see page 000)
+ Engaging in risky behavior (violence, sexual promiscuity, illegal actions)
+ Pretending it isn't there or you don't feel it
+ Defacing, destroying, or discarding belongings or mementos of your loved one, which will be impossible to replace once you cool down

Look at the list and see what applies to you. If you need help in dealing with your anger, then ask someone for help. Share your feelings. Many community groups, therapists, and support groups can help you discuss and diffuse your anger.

One of the therapeutic techniques I recommend is the following: Get a tennis racquet or baseball bat. Set a timer for five minutes. Take the racquet or bat and hit the soft part of your bed or sofa. Imagine the anger discharging itself with each swing. When the timer goes off, or if you stop before, tell yourself that you have helped yourself get rid of some of your anger without actually hurting anyone. Rest. You may feel exhausted after this exercise.

Use the power of physical exercise as an outlet for your anger. Physical movement helps to you to get the anger out of your body and discharge it without hurting anyone. Jennifer offers another exercise:

> I was so angry, I couldn't eat or sleep. I knew I had to do something before it destroyed me. I got a punching bag and had it attached to the ceiling. I put gloves on and punched it over and over until I couldn't anymore. It helped me more than I realized—I still do it when I need a healthy release.

There are many ways to channel your anger, and it is crucial to recognize that anger is a natural part of your grief, something that needs to be listened to and then let go of.

Addictive Behaviors

GRIEF CAN LEAD us to engage in behaviors that can have devastating effects on our lives, our relationships, and our health. Addiction, whether to drugs, alcohol, work, sex, gambling, or other behaviors, often develop as a response to our grief—and the extreme pain we are feeling. While some behaviors may work to calm or distract you, and may actually be helpful, many are not and need to be identified and changed where necessary. Richard whose wife, Susan, was murdered, found himself engaging in the following behavior:

> I always worked a lot but, after Susan died, I wanted to work all the time. It gave me relief, except when memories of her broke through. But much of the time, I just literally buried myself in my work. The trouble was I was not there for my kids or myself. I had to stop working all the time and face what happened.

Ultimately, Richard cut his work hours. He took the time to grieve, instead of avoiding his feelings. He also found more time to be with his children and help them with their feelings of loss. His family grew closer rather than further apart, and together they were able to grieve their loss fully. This enabled them to move toward in their healing instead of away from it. Although Richard could have become a workaholic, he recognized it as an escape from his grief, and took steps to become more present with his family.

Drug and/or alcohol use coupled with extreme grief can create problems. Culturally, getting drunk to drown one's sorrows is an acceptable remedy. However, many people use substances to deal with pain and then become addicted. It complicates an already complex situation because it masks feelings and keeps us from doing the hard work of grief. Substances, including prescribed medications, keep us mired in a vicious cycle from which we cannot recover.

Jason, who was twenty-three when I met him, had lost his father when he was sixteen. He told me the following:

> When my dad died, I freaked. My dad and I did everything together; he was my hero. I shut down inside. I started drinking and smoking pot to get rid of the feelings. Everything I did was about the drugs. I didn't have a sober thought for years. When I hit bottom, I went to AA, stopped using, and had to learn another way of dealing with the pain. It wasn't easy but, eventually, it worked.

While there is nothing wrong with wanting some relief from your grief, don't allow a substance or behavior to take over your life. How can you tell if you have a problem? Ask yourself the following questions:

+ Does your life revolve around your substance or behavior? (procuring it, using it, recovering from it)
+ Does it have a compulsive quality about it? (You can't wait to use it, get frustrated if you don't have it, or have withdrawal if you stop.)
+ Does it cause you to miss work, isolate from your family, and cause arguments?
+ Does your personality change when using? (For example, when you drink, do you become mean or nasty? Irresponsible?)
+ Do you black out? (not remember what you did, where you left the car, etc.)
+ When you use a substance or an action (gambling, sex, etc.), do you engage in risky behavior? (spend too much, put yourself in dangerous situations, lose control?)
+ Were you ever hospitalized or treated for it?

If you answered yes to any of these questions—yes, even just one—you need to take steps to end or forestall a dangerous addiction. Please consider getting help or talking to someone about it. You will complicate an already difficult situation by indulging in addictive behavior. *Don't run the risk of destroying yourself and allowing an addiction to affect your loved ones . . . who are still very much alive and with you.*

Family Members Grieve Differently

IN BOTH MY professional and personal experience, I have seen how different members of our families handle grief. My children, Anna and Mike, had their own ways of handling Aaron's death, which were different than mine. Also, children and young adults will deal with grief differently than will mature adults. Their sense of immortality is profoundly affected. Young people often think of themselves as indestructible, but trauma changes that by bringing them face to face with destruction and death. Often young people may hide their feelings and use drugs and alcohol, as Jason did. They have not developed coping skills for grief, but then why would they? We raise our children for life, not death. We spend our time protecting them from such things, yet trauma can change that safety in an instant.

Siblings, even as adults, may feel protective toward their parents and not express their grief openly, in fear of upsetting them, as Jennifer did:

> I felt like my mother's pain was much worse than mine. After all, Gary was her only son. I did not want to make her suffering any worse than it already was. Now, years later, I realize that I needed help—but I thought about others before myself. Even now, I find it hard to talk about what happened because I don't want to upset anyone—and the truth is, I don't really know how to talk about it.

If you have children or siblings who are grieving, try to open up a dialogue with them, and give them space to talk to you. But remember you are all experiencing grief in your own way and may not be able to support one another as well as you would like. A technique that can be used for your family is the open discussion model, where all of the members who wish to participate set aside a time to be with one another and support one another. In this technique, one person begins the discussion with a statement about the way he or she feels, but with the ground rule that no one may put anyone else on the spot. Participants are allowed to "pass" if their turn comes to speak, but they do not wish to. My children and I did this the summer Aaron died. We sat around the table:

"I feel lonely without Aaron," I began.

"I was thinking about him today," Anna said.

"I miss him," Mike said.

I asked the next question: "Do you want to talk about it?" If the answer was no, we moved on. Sometimes no one wanted to talk and we closed the meeting after a few minutes. Sometimes, though, one of us would share a memory or tell a story.

This family meeting has the advantage of offering support while also respecting personal boundaries and privacy. It helps each one of you know what's going on in your minds and hearts instead of isolating from each other. The meeting lets everyone know you are all going through this together in whatever way you can, and in ways that may be quite different. Do not pressure anyone to contribute who does not wish to talk. Sometimes just gathering around a table is enough. Although, for my family, it was painful in the beginning because we were so aware of the big gaping hole that would have been Aaron's presence.

GRANDPARENTS OR OTHER elderly members of the family, even if they have already been through the loss of other loved ones, are grieving afresh, too, and often their grief is compounded by age and ill health. They, too, need to talk about their trauma and to both receive and lend assistance. Often, because of their age, they may have the wisdom that younger people do not, and can offer advice and support that will be valuable to all. They may also be seeking now to understand a violent act that makes particularly little sense to people of their generation and values. If they are willing and available and everyone agrees, then ask them to participate in family meetings.

IF THERE ARE young children involved they, too, will need special consideration. Obviously, young children are not familiar with the concept of death, but they will know that something is happening and that people around them are upset to a magnitude they may never have witnessed.

They will pick up pieces of information without necessarily understanding how to fit them together, and be frightened not only by what is going on but by how they are mistakenly interpreting the situation. Not explaining what has happened may be more terrifying to them than presenting the simple truth. Also, asking them what *they* think happened may help to shed crucial light on misunderstandings, such as their belief that their being angry with the victim somehow caused his or her death. Do take the time to make sure they have a source of comfort and stability. For example, many people will arrange for their young children to go to a trusted relative or neighbor, perhaps the family of a close playmate of the child.

If that is what you choose to do, make sure you have a conversation with your child before he or she goes. You can say the following: "We are sad because something happened to____. It isn't because of anything you did. But you don't have to worry, we are taking care of it. You are going to go to _____ . Everything will be all right—and I will talk to you soon."

Many people either choose to keep their children close by or do not have a place for the youngsters to go. If that is the case, try to enlist the help of a friend or family member to be with the child, offering comfort and security to him or her within your own home environment.

You may have to explain the concept of death to your child, when time and conditions permit. This is very difficult to do, but there are books written to help you and also children's books that you can read to your young ones. Please see the appendix for more information about these.

You will also have to decide whether to have your child attend the funeral or memorial service. This is a very personal decision, one which you may ask your family members, clergy, or funeral director to help you make.

PLEASE DO USE your support network to help one another grieve. Family members may elect to pursue different forms of therapy, as suits their individual personality. These techniques are not one-size-fits-all, that need be done *en masse* or not at all; use whatever works. Avail yourselves of the community support groups, therapists, and organizations discussed in the appendix at the end of this book.

A remarkable book about family healing after loss is Alice Sebold's novel, *The Lovely Bones*. This is a story about what happens in the lives of a family when a child is killed. It is a beautiful story and one that inspired me. It paints a picture of how each of us will grieve in our own way and how we need to have understanding and compassion for one another.

Grieving does not exempt us from standard gender roles. Men generally grieve differently than do women. In our culture, men are taught to not show their emotions; historically, women are the ones who are encouraged to openly grieve, while men are supposed to be pillars of strength. Women will show emotions, talk about them, and share them with family and friends. Women are also often the ones who take care of the funeral arrangements, the food, and other people. Traditionally, men hold their emotions inside, and retreat to hide their wounds. They will work more, drink more, or simply not talk about the situation. This is a dangerous way of dealing with grief and loss. These deep feelings need to be expressed or at least acknowledged. Sometimes, suppressing such strong feelings can result in illness, heart trouble, and addictions. Many men report feelings of depression, and lose their connections with their family, and sometimes, their lives, after a traumatic experience. Richard shared with me how he felt after Susan's death:

> What was I supposed to do? Break down crying? I was not used to expressing my feelings. I guess I was taught that men had to be strong and not show emotion, because that was a sign of weakness. I felt like I had to be in control and that crying didn't do any good. But what I realized, not only was I working too much, I was unable to feel anything. I felt dead inside. I knew I had to open up, but I didn't know how. When I began to show my feelings, I learned that I wasn't being weak; on the contrary, I was being strong enough to let other people know how I felt.

Often, men will become preoccupied with either catching the perpetrator or thinking about what he wants to do once he does. Men have long been in the role of protector and avenger, and when this right is taken out of their control, the desire for justice can become personal—and all-consuming. But times are changing for men, and they are recognizing the value of sharing experiences, rather than withdrawing. It is not a sign of weakness to grieve, but rather a willingness to share feelings and move through them is a means to regain strength.

Birthdays, holidays, and anniversaries

THE FIRST YEAR after the loss of a loved one is especially difficult because we are experiencing the first round of significant dates since the trauma happened. Holidays, birthdays, and anniversaries will "trigger" us and at these times the waves of grief will become stronger. Until you have gone through an entire cycle of a year, you won't know how you will react.

August 14, 1999, was Aaron's twenty-first birthday—had he lived. Anna's nineteenth birthday was the day before, August 13. How would I, during my intense mourning, both honor her birthday and the very next day deal with the fact that my son was dead? We celebrated Anna's birthday with a cake and pink roses; the next day, Anna and Mike and many of Aaron's friends went to the New Jersey shore for Aaron's birthday. I stayed behind.

Several weeks before, Aaron's friends had gone to the house on McDowell Avenue in Steubenville and gathered his belongings—I couldn't do that during the week I was there; it was just too painful. Aaron didn't have much, mostly clothes and keepsakes. They sat there in boxes; I hadn't been able to bring myself to go through them. The night of Aaron's birthday, I rummaged through the boxes. I saw his sneakers, a red baseball cap with the letter *A* on it, a small crucifix, and a term paper with his scratchy writing on it. Among his belongings was a CD of mine that I hadn't seen since our trip home to Philadelphia from Colorado the summer before.

I went into my living room, the same room where we had gathered only months before while we waited for news about Aaron. I lit a candle, and put on the CD I had found. I drifted into thoughts of my son and his birthday, and heard the following words: "Please remember me . . ." It was a song of yearning for one who is lost and a plea to always remember him.

As I listened, the agony of my grief returned, choking me. But after it passed, I felt peace. Aaron was speaking to me. Even in death, he was there, telling me to remember him. And how would I ever forget? Life and death are two sides of the same world, one seen and the other unseen. When we lose someone we love, we live in both, celebrating and grieving. I blew out the candle and said goodnight.

When the birthday of your loved one approaches, realize you will not know what to do—how could you; you haven't done this before. Many times, the anticipation of the day is harder than the actual day. Rita said the following:

I was upset thinking about Don's birthday months before. By the time it came, I was exhausted. I cried and slept through most of it. That was the best I could do.

You will need to find ways of passing significant dates, especially those relating to the loss of your loved one. You will find yourself thinking about it and mourning anew long before the day arrives. If you can, plan to have someone with you who can help you. You may find you are unable to do much of anything, or you may want to do something simple, like lighting a candle or visiting the person's gravesite. The day is bound to be a sad day—an inevitable result of your loss. Yet it is better to realize it will be hard, but that this day will pass—and perhaps next year will be different. When the date arrives, try any of these suggestions:

+ Realize it is only one day—albeit a long one.
+ Go to the cemetery and bring flowers and balloons if you want to.
+ Spend part of the day or all of it with someone you like.
+ Light a candle and blow it out, making a wish for the one you love.
+ Write in your journal.
+ Rent movies and watch them.
+ Sleep.
+ Go for a walk.
+ Do something for someone else.
+ Remember the birthdays you shared with your loved one; no one can take them from you.

The first round of traditional holidays is torturous for most survivors of a death, even when it had not been violent. While everyone is planning to get together and celebrate with their loved ones, you are missing yours and wondering how you will ever get through such days.

That first year, for my family, Anna had started college in Manhattan in the fall and would be home for Christmas. She had immersed herself in her college studies and did well, but the shadow of her brother's death was never far from her. Michael was a sophomore at West Catholic High School. I was grateful to the staff at West; they supported Mike when I was barely able to. He was so young to experience such trauma; first his father, now his brother. I worried about them. I felt guilty that I could not protect them or Aaron from what had happened.

On Christmas day Anna, Michael, and I gathered in the living room, trying to be cheery when, really, none of us felt like celebrating Christmas. We were tender to one another, acutely aware of how much we missed Aaron. We tried to pretend he was there but knew he wasn't. It was just hard to even say his name. The space where he would have been was so huge, it was unbearably painful.

Somehow, we muddled through. We decorated the tree quickly, as if we just wanted to get it over with. I had the strange sensation of everything being in slow motion; each time I placed an ornament on the tree, it seemed so heavy. One of my cousins had made a wooden ornament in the shape of a tree, with four smiling stars and each of our names on it, with the year 1999. I placed it right in front of our Christmas tree, in some kind of triumph that we were still a family and that no one, no event, would ever change that.

Earlier, I had tried to buy Christmas cards. I picked up one box that showed an angel standing on top of the world, with the stars and moon around her. It read, "Peace on Earth." I felt myself swaying; I felt the waves of grief closing in on me. I was afraid they would hit and I would start crying. I put the cards back and ran out of the store.

As holidays approach, extra care needs to be taken with ourselves and others. Every personal tradition we used to love sharing with the departed becomes a potential minefield. As Lea felt on first New Year's without her husband, Dave,

The first year was the worst. Especially at New Year's.
Dave and I always talked about the past year and the
good things that happened—we always looked forward
to the new year and would think of what we wanted to
do. New Year's Eve, he wasn't there. He was murdered
in December; that's what happened for us that year. I
couldn't bear it; I cried myself to sleep and wanted it to
all go away. Mercifully, it did.

Often in the first year, we try to hold on to our traditions
because they are the remnants of the life we used to have and it is
too soon to create new ones. In fact, for many of us, just holding it
together the first round of holidays is a victory; we will have to wait
for time to make us strong enough to create new traditions.

Using all of your resources, you will have to try to do the best
you can, and have compassion for yourself and your family. Do what
you can, and if you do nothing, that is fine, too. Do not allow the
expectations of others to pressure you into doing things you are not
prepared to handle. Rather, allow your feelings to dictate what you
will do. Do not expect too much of the day—it, too, will pass. The
following are some suggestions for you to pass the first holidays:

+ At Thanksgiving, make a toast to your loved one and thank him/
  her for all the wonderful Thanksgivings you shared together.
+ Ask everybody to share something brief about a memory they
  are thankful for.
+ On other holidays, think of giving a gift or charitable contribution in the name of your loved one. Or help someone else who
  is worse off than you.

Give thanks for those of your family who are still with you and
know that your loved one remains with you in your memories. You
will always have those to revisit, in your own special family reunion
of the heart.

DEALING WITH THE first anniversary of the violent event is another challenge. By the time spring came, in the year 2000, I was looking forward to the flowers, the dogwoods, and the cherry trees. It was lovely. I breathed in the beauty; life was bursting out all over. The axiom I have always lived by is: even in the most barren desert, there is still some beauty to behold; the task is to find it.

A year had passed since I last saw Aaron and this first spring without him was bittersweet. Here again was the paradox. While I did see the beauty, I missed him so much—I was being tossed by the waves of grief again. I was overwhelmed by the reality that, a year ago, the world had been this beautiful when I last saw him.

By the time the anniversary came, at the end of May, I was drained and worn out. The day passed and I was grateful I'd gotten through one whole year. If I had done that, surely I could do it again. At the same time, I wondered how I could go through another year without Aaron. I realized both my strength and my fragility: I knew that, as long as I lived, I would always have this grief with me in the springtime. Softer, I hoped, but it would always be there.

Olivia lost her two children in an automobile accident caused by a drunk driver. She had this to say about the first anniversary:

> I was afraid for two months before the anniversary. I was afraid I wasn't going to make it. I literally thought I would lose my mind and do something really crazy. My husband felt the same way, but he was quieter about it. When the anniversary came, we held each other—holding on for what, we weren't sure. We were numb, just waiting for the day to be over. It did pass, but it seemed so long. I was just glad it was over, and so was Chris.

For you, the first anniversary will be a hard day among many hard days. As with birthdays, the anticipation of the event often is harder than the actual day. You may be so exhausted from anticipating the sorrow days before, you will be worn out by the time the date actually comes. Whatever the case may be for you, try and have someone with you that day. Do not do it alone. Ask for help.

 IF YOU ARE a friend or relative, and a holiday, birthday, or the anniversary of a traumatic event is approaching, please reach out and be there.

Take the person out, or send a note, or call on the phone. Whatever you can do, it will be appreciated and needed. Remember to reach out to other family members or friends of the deceased as well. All of you will be handling this day in your own way, but you can offer one another comfort and solace. You who are left behind are joined together by what has happened. If you can, plan to be together on the day. Offer each other love and care. Acknowledge how hard it is. Work together to create a new tradition that honors the person on this date.

Hopefully, you will be able to say that, after a year, the most intense waves of grief will have subsided, and you will have learned how to read the signs of when a storm is coming. I hope, too, that as you make your passage through difficult emotions, you discover the kindness of family, friends, and even strangers. For now, you have done well. Take a breath, and rest.

Stage 5

Out in the Deep

PRACTICING THE THREE PRINCIPLES

AFTER THE FIRST year of your grief, the intense waves may have subsided and become more predictable. You will now have some idea of when they are coming, what triggers them, and how to keep from drowning. Certainly, your emotions can still overwhelm you, and are by no means insignificant. However, after the first year, you will have gone through one complete cycle of holidays and anniversaries, and hopefully will have gained some mastery over your feelings. Stage 5 will help you understand what happens after you have learned how to ride the initial waves that forced you out into the deep part of the ocean.

For many, this is a dangerous time. Reality and consequences sink in. The shock and numbness have worn off and you realize, sadly, that you will be confronted with the consequences of your trauma for a long time, if not the rest of your life. You may now experience less volatile but more profound feelings of anger, despair, and abandonment. People don't talk about your loved ones anymore. You may feel out of sync with everyone else in the world—they have moved on with their lives, while you have not. You may find it hard to relate to others because they tell you that you should move on, get over it, live life—all well-meant suggestions that wound you deeply. Often, this is the time when survivors experience depression and may even have suicidal thoughts. You may feel that you have been left behind by your loved one and that you cannot catch up. You are in limbo between your old, pretrauma world and the new one you have yet to discover. You are far from the shore of the life you once knew—you can see it behind you, but as much as you want to, you now know you cannot go back. You may feel abandoned by both the living and the dead.

Many people have told me that they needed more help after the first year because living every day with the reality of what had happened was so difficult. Sharon said the following about stage 5:

> The first year after Jack was murdered was horrible, full of crying and huge ups and downs. But people were around and talked about him. His memory was still fresh and some of him seemed still alive. But after the first year, people said less, came over less. Jack seemed to disappear from everyone's life, except mine. I felt so abandoned. I almost wished it was the first year again. At least I felt something; now it seemed like I was dead, too.

You may feel stuck, anchored, unable to move forward. And rightly so—you are still grieving and, as much as you and everyone else would like to achieve closure, you cannot. This word *closure* is one which I and many other survivors detest. There is no "closure." This grief like no other will be a life-long journey. People will insist we have closure, because they think it will be better for us and for them.

It is crucial to remember this is your grief and it will take as long as it needs. There is no way to will "getting over" these things. Nothing will change the fact that your loved one met a violent end. However, there are things that can help you navigate the deepest part of the ocean. I have found that there are three principles, which have helped me and others I have worked with over the years. They are: acceptance, forgiveness, and gratitude.

Acceptance asks us to recognize what we can change and what we cannot—and ask for the wisdom to understand the difference. Forgiveness helps us to work on our feelings of anger, hatred, and revenge, which inevitably harm us more than the person to whom they are directed. Gratitude helps us recognize what has been given, taken away, and remains after the storms have passed.

These principles are not easy, nor are they meant to be. You will accept, forgive, and be grateful in different ways, according to your own circumstances and temperament. There are no demands here, only that you have a willingness to consider these principles in your own time, in your way. These three principles will be tested throughout the stages of your journey and your life—they develop and change as you do, with time and patience. But before I present a detailed description of each principle, I want to talk about how to cope with the legal system.

I have chosen to talk about it here in stage 5, because while you might have faced an arraignment early in the perpetration of a crime, the trial itself usually does not take place in the first year. Even if there is not a trial, the legal system will investigate homicides. In a suicide, traffic or other accident, or drug overdose, the police will be involved as well. Lawyers and judges may be needed to settle an estate or establish guardianship of a minor. Regardless of the particulars, the death of your loved one will very likely involve the legal system—which, unto itself, can be painful, frustrating, discouraging, and ultimately will require you to call upon all of your resources.

Following a violent crime, where the perpetrator has been apprehended, there will be a trial (unless a plea bargain is reached). Depending on your relationship with the victim, you may be expected to face the perpetrator and sit through the horrible details all over again. Plus, you may hear or have to look at additional evidence that may be new to you, and very distressing.

I'll tell you how the trials were for me. After the first anniversary of Aaron's death, the second summer came and, with it, the trials of Nathan Herring and Terrell Yarbrough. I made the trip once again to Steubenville and as I drove on Route 22, I wondered, with a shudder, where Aaron had been murdered. I hadn't visited the site. I couldn't. During the first year of grief, I had struggled so much with my inner "torturers," I couldn't fully face how he died. I had compartmentalized my grief, focusing on the immediacy of my loss of Aaron, expecting I would have to deal with the trial later. I knew some of the details, but during the first year, it was more than enough to know he had been woken up, beaten, taken to a dark hillside, and shot in the head.

The trials took place in the small courthouse in Steubenville. Many of Aaron and Brian's friends came to be with our two families. I heard testimony of how Herring and Yarbrough broke into the house on McDowell Avenue while Aaron and Brian were sleeping, surprising them, and beating them. They broke Aaron's jaw with the gun they had brought with them. Andrew, who shared the house, was upstairs and heard the ruckus. He jumped out of his window and looked into the window of the living room. He saw someone wearing a mask, and shouted for Aaron and Brian. He then ran to a house three doors away and called the police. In the time that elapsed, Herring and Yarbrough allegedly herded Aaron and Brian into the back seat of Brian's black Chevy blazer and sped off toward Route 22. It was reported that they then took the boys to the woods, shot them, and walked away, leaving the bodies under two white, wild rose bushes.

After all the evidence was presented in both trials and the final arguments made, the jury went out to deliberate; we went to the hotel to wait until they had reached a decision. When we were called back, we rushed to the courtroom and I nervously awaited the verdict. Both Nathan Herring and Terrell Yarbrough were found guilty.

After the trials were over, we once again left Steubenville. I was on my way back home, feeling wounded and sick, yet glad it was over. The murderers had been sentenced. Now, I could continue my journey of grief with the trials behind me . . . or so I thought. But the torturers returned. Because I had heard the hard evidence of the trials, and had been forced to spend time in the courtroom with Aaron's murderers, I was now feeling the reality of what actually happened to him—and it was killing me. It sent me into the deepest part of the ocean, clinging to whatever life preservers I had while they, too, were being ravaged.

A trial involving a loved one will be one of the most awful experiences you will ever endure. You are made to relive everything, hear details you never knew, and place the entire process in the hands of the justice system. You have no idea how it will turn out: Will there be justice, or will the perpetrators be found not guilty? What will the defendant's lawyers and the media say about your loved ones? Will the truth be heard, or will lies be told? Anyone who has endured this knows what I am talking about—how very often, the victim is put on trial as well as his or her family. It is an awful thing to realize that all of this is taken out of your hands and left to a system in which justice may or may not prevail. Nonetheless, it is the best system we have and, for very many of us, justice will indeed prevail. For that, I am grateful.

I want to mention here that everyone in the prosecutor's office in Steubenville did their very best to help us get through these awful trials. They fought for justice for Aaron and Brian. Every day during the trial, they and Teresa Laman, of the Victims Advocate Office helped us in every way they could—and for that I will always be grateful.

If you are preparing for a trial, you will want whatever support you can gather for these events. The emotional challenges will be many. You will have to endure much more than you ever thought possible. You will hear things you won't believe and be wounded in ways from which you will not soon recover. You will need to gather your strength and courage. You should have your family and friends close by you for this ordeal. Make sure, whenever you must encounter anything to do with the legal system, there is either someone accompanying you or someone you can call. You will need someone to talk to, to guide you through not only what you are hearing, but the enormous stress of your feelings.

Sometimes There Is No Justice

UNFORTUNATELY, SOME WILL not experience justice. This is the ongoing agony following a violent crime. Not only has a loved one been viciously murdered or harmed, but you may have to deal with a court decision that seems unfair—a "nonguilty" verdict, a light sentence, a plea bargain that allows a perpetrator to slip through legal loopholes. Another side of this is that, in some cases, the perpetrator is never arrested, there is no trial. For the survivors, there is yet another, different ocean of grief. Gordon, whose son was murdered, shared,

> Matt was murdered in a robbery. They never caught the person. It is incredible that we live in a country where someone can murder another person and not get caught. I have tried everything from hiring a private detective to questioning everyone in that neighborhood—but came up empty. No one saw anything. Or so they said. I have had to live with this. I used to think about it all the time—wondering if this person could be the one. I was always thinking of how I would catch the criminal and what I would do. It was destroying me. It did, it killed a part of me.

Gordon's story is all too familiar to us; if the criminal is never caught or is released by the legal system, family and friends have to learn to live with the reality that the person who did this to their loved one is out there, free.

Sometimes, the body of the victim is never recovered. I have spoken to people whose grief is compounded by the fact that they cannot find the one they love. Ken said this about his sister, Rowan:

> We knew Rowan was murdered. We found her clothes, her backpack. We searched for two weeks, and there was no trace of her. It's been five years and there are no new leads. For us, the search for Rowan has never stopped. We are always looking for Rowan. I dream of finding her again, and then I wake up and nothing has changed. Sometimes I think she might still be alive. This will never be closed for me, I'll always be looking.

These cases are particularly painful, as are those in which we have personally seen or been told about the physical damage that has been done to a loved one's body. This is the grief like no other—the repercussions caused by an act of violence upon someone we love. And for many of us, we will be faced with the grief of violence that our loved one did to his or her own body, or a drug overdose or lethal accident—all of these circumstances bring us into the horror of a violent death—one which plunges us into the deepest part of the ocean.

We will need to use everything we have learned to navigate this stage—and must learn even more.

The Three Principles

IN STAGE 2, you saw how you must step up and do what life asks of you. You cannot avoid your suffering, but you do have a choice of how you will do the hard work of grief. The three principles of acceptance, forgiveness, and gratitude can help you. Without these principles, your journey may be much more dangerous and difficult. Remember, these are skills are learned; they don't always come naturally.

ACCEPTANCE

Acceptance was always a struggle for me, even before Aaron's death. I believe it is for many of us. After all, who wants to accept things that are painful, or that we feel are wrong? Who wants to believe we can't control things for ourselves and those we love?

Human nature wants to take charge and make sure nothing bad happens. We want what we want, when we want it, and we certainly do not want to lose, whether that loss is a loved one, or our marriage, job, house, money, or health. How do we reconcile this desire to control with the reality of what life brings to us? I have found that the well-known serenity prayer provides some excellent guidelines for learning about acceptance:

> God, grant me the serenity to accept the things I
>   cannot change
> The courage to change the things I can
> And the wisdom to know the difference

A note here: some of you may not want to use a prayer—perhaps you are too angry, feel uncomfortable with this prayer, or don't believe in prayer itself. However, these words have become a part of our culture—secular and spiritual. So, please, try and use them, in whatever way you are able to.

"God, grant me the serenity to accept the things I cannot change"

This line tells us to ask someone or something which is outside of ourself for serenity. It tells us it's a request. It's not something we immediately possess, especially in our grief—we will need to reach out to someone or something which is larger than ourselves to help us find peace. Violence is the opposite of serenity—and will challenge any peace we have or will have in our lives. Many of you will find your belief in God will help you ask and receive serenity to accept the things you cannot change. For others, you may not believe this or have lost your faith. Gordon's story helps to illuminate this:

> After Matt was shot, I was obsessed with finding his
> killer. It became my focus in life. I shut out everybody. I

was agitated and angry all the time—it was destroying my marriage and my family. I had to calm myself down or lose even more. How was I supposed to calm down, where the person who murdered my son was still out there?

Gordon struggled with this question and realized he could not continue to live this way. He did not believe in prayer—but he did relate to having peace, or balance, in his life. He was willing to try. Gordon recognized that he had to stop thinking all the time about catching the criminal. He had to accept the face that he might not find Matt's killer. After acknowledging that his focus on the killer was preventing him from feeling other emotions such as grief and sorrow, Gordon started to reach out to get help. He had to reach outside of himself to get help. He talked to his wife about his feelings of powerlessness, agitation, and obsession. He told her how he felt impotent because he couldn't protect their son—and how, if he caught the person who did it, he thought he would be in control again. Slowly, Gordon began to understand that he wanted peace—and that was more important than his obsession with taking back control. Instead of focusing on Matt's killer, he began to focus on his family. Gordon also allowed himself to feel and express his feelings, such as rage and sorrow. Working with a therapist, he tried techniques that would help him release negative energy. For example, when he grew agitated, he went to the gym and worked out his aggressions. Instead of keeping everything bottled up, he made a commitment to talk to his wife, his therapist, and a close male friend. Gordon also had to come to terms with the fact that he was powerless over what happened to Matt. This was the most painful part of all—it wasn't easy, and it didn't happen overnight. He struggled with acceptance for along time—but it started to work, he eventually gained more peace in his life.

If you are struggling with acceptance try the following:

Using your journal, write down the things over which you are powerless. These things will already be present in your story—the violence, the death, the details. Review them and admit that, no matter what you do, you will never be able to change them, ever.

Then ask yourself what is more important in your life: serenity, or not accepting your powerlessness. Simply put, you must recognize that there are some things you cannot change. Ask for the serenity to accept the things you cannot change—believe that someone or something outside of yourself can help you—whether that is your faith, spiritual belief, a friend or someone you trust.

The journey through loss is very much one of acceptance, however the loss occurred. That the loss involved sudden violence makes this a hard task, and it will take time to master. And the only way we can begin to move forward is to acknowledge and accept what has happened.

When I gave a keynote speech at the Compassionate Friends anniversary dinner, there was an older man present who had lost his son many years before. I remember him saying this: "Until we learn acceptance, there will be no peace in our lives."

How will you do this? First of all, recognize that acceptance is not something that happens overnight. It is a change in your way of thinking, one which you may rebel against, or reject. Tara said the following about acceptance:

> There was no way I could accept what happened to my sister, she didn't deserve what happened to her. I kept trying to imagine what I could have done to change it for her. It was consuming me, day and night. I tried the serenity prayer and couldn't do it. Finally, I had to realize, I was powerless to change anything that happened to Vicki. I stopped fighting it—I accepted it and I guess that was the beginning of some kind of peace.

Ask yourself if you want peace in your life. If you answer yes, you are on your way to realizing that acceptance is a skill you will need. You must ask yourself if you are willing to develop it. The key is willingness, which is all you need to move forward. Using your resources is important here. When you are agitated, you need to do something to move the energy out of your mind and body. This can be as simple as taking a walk or doing an intense workout. Meditation, yoga, and prayer are excellent skills to learn and use for this purpose. Here is another simple exercise: Try saying to yourself, "I am willing to accept what I cannot change; I am powerless to change_____" (whatever applies to your situation).

You need to come to terms with your powerlessness, which is the opposite of control. This is a very tall order for most of us. How do we abandon our control and admit powerlessness? The answer is that we simply do. The paradox here is that, the moment you realize you cannot change what has happened; you are then free to accept it. You need to trust that the sense of release you will feel shall empower you, not weaken you. When you stop fighting the ocean, then you can move out of the deep.

"The courage to change the things I can"

This tells us that, while we are powerless over some things, there are things we *can* change. But we will need courage, the first of the eight qualities, to be willing to change the things we can. Those "things" are usually ourselves and the way we think. We can change how we look at and respond to events over which we have no control.

After Aaron's death, people asked, "Why Aaron?" I struggled; I asked that question, too. Why my wonderful son, Aaron—he was a good person—why him?

The answer was painful: why *not* Aaron? Is my child more precious than anyone else's? These terrible things happen to us as human beings no matter who we are. Death and violence, sadly, are some of the only things that aren't prejudiced—anyone can be affected, any time. Goodness or innocence or how important a person is has nothing to do with it.

I had to change the way I thought. I believed that since I was good and my children were good, no bad things would happen to us. It was a painful realization that bad things happen to everyone because that is the way life is. There was no use blaming God for taking my son. Instead, I realized we live in a world when the laws of love are broken every day in every way, from the simple disservice we do each other to the brutal murders we watch on the evening news. I saw this in our humanity—how we as humans do such unbelievably terrible things—*this* was the real tragedy, not what God did or did not do.

It was difficult to change my perception and expectations of the world I lived in. But if I was to have any peace at all, I would have to find the courage to change what I could—myself. Abbey shared the following with me after her son, Ben, was abandoned at a hospital after a drug overdose:

> I couldn't accept that Ben would never be the same. He was alive, but the brain damage was so severe, he wasn't anything like he was. I kept trying to change him and get him to be what I wanted, which was the Ben I knew. I had to find the courage within myself to change what I wanted and deal with the fact of what happened. I changed myself, and found the courage to accept and love him for who he was now.

In your own life, look for what you have the power to change. Use the following examples:

+ Although you are powerless to change what has happened, where can you bring about change now?
+ Can you change the way you think about what happened?
+ Can you change your attitude toward life from the despair you may be feeling to hope, if only for a moment?

Jane's story sheds some more light on change and acceptance:

> I hated the world and people in it for what it did to me, to my brother. He was attacked and killed because of

what he was; it was a hate crime. I realized that my hatred was keeping me stuck in a dark hole and I was becoming like the people who murdered my brother. I had to find the strength and courage to change the way I thought about the world, or it would destroy me.

Jane came to realize that she was being damaged by her own thoughts and the hatred she was feeling. The change had to come from her—not the other way around. You, too, will find things you can change about yourself. Think about where you might be harboring this hatred of the world that took your loved one. Can you change this kind of thinking into something more kind, patient, charitable? I am not asking you to don rose-colored glasses, but to develop a real, practical way of looking at life. You need to make changes in order to survive, and since the only thing you truly have power over is yourself, you have to start there.

The last of the human freedoms is to choose how we will suffer. That surely means having the courage to change ourselves.

"The wisdom to know the difference"

We develop wisdom through our experiences in life. We learn what we can control and what we cannot. Wisdom knows when to give up, accept, and courageously live on. It chooses its battles well, not ceaselessly fighting or railing against what cannot be changed. As Krista said,

> The first year after Katy's death almost killed me. I didn't want to live. I fought every day against what happened. I couldn't accept it and there was no peace. I was stuck treading water. I started to think about the serenity prayer, and wisdom. I didn't know what that meant, but I did start thinking realistically about what I could and couldn't change—and accepting that, maybe that was the beginning of wisdom.

Wisdom simply means that you begin to discern what you can change and what you cannot. A wise person does not fight the waves, but instead finds a way to move with them. Without wisdom, we are always fighting, never understanding the value of peace and never finding it. No one can fight forever, without eventually drowning.

The following exercise will help you to learn how to move with the waves: Visualize yourself out in the deep, treading water. You are tired and weary of the struggle, but you don't know what else to do. You are afraid to let go because you think you will drown. You fight and fight instead of accepting what happened to bring you here. Now take a deep, deep breath. Stop struggling. Realize you can be wise; you can stop fighting the ocean. You know what you can change and what you cannot. You can have peace by letting go. You will float and be carried to a new, calmer place.

You can do this exercise every day, it will help you gain acceptance, courage, and wisdom in your life.

FORGIVENESS

The second principle is the most difficult for me. While I recognize that forgiveness is powerful and has many benefits, its practice presents many challenges to me. While I may be able to forgive something done to me, I am not sure I can forgive something done to someone else. I question whether it is my right to forgive a harm done to someone else. I cannot forgive Aaron's murderers for taking Aaron's life. That life was his, not mine to give or take; therefore I cannot forgive someone for taking what is not mine to begin with. Intellectually, I may be able to understand why the murderers may have committed this crime—their history, life, and circumstances combined for a volatile reaction—yet I cannot fathom forgiving the act itself, and find myself asking the question, Are there some acts which are unforgivable? To this day, I struggle with achieving forgiveness; I cannot seem to bring myself to do it. It is not because I don't want to, it's because I cannot. It seems too large an idea for me. You would probably expect as a therapist I would be telling you that you should forgive. How can I tell you to do something I myself have not done?

Shortly after Aaron's death, people I didn't know sent me books on forgiveness. While I am sure they had good intentions, I felt pressured to do something I hadn't begun to think about, and certainly hadn't arrived at. Each of us needs to approach forgiveness at our own pace. What is good for one person may not be for another. I know that the issue of forgiveness is ahead for me, but I can honestly say, without reproach for myself, that I am not there and may never be. However, I do believe that forgiveness and anger are related. While I still struggle with forgiveness, I cannot allow my anger to go unchecked. Therefore, I have taken the position that anger should be dealt with first, and then forgiveness.

Many survivors will say that they are confronted by the raw force of anger when they experience trials or parole hearings or any of the legal challenges associated with the violence done to their loved ones. Anger is a powerful emotion. You may find yourself doing and thinking things that you would never considering doing.

I felt like strangling the men who stood trial for Aaron and Brian's murders. I felt like making them suffer for what they did to Aaron. But what good would that do? It was up to me to confront my feelings and not allow them to destroy me. I felt sick from anger; it was infecting me with its poison. I realized that I could not allow it to go unchecked, but had to move through it so it would not hurt myself or others. I used the techniques I told you about in stage 4, and pounded out my anger. I took walks in the woods and threw stones and rocks. I wanted to break every window in my house—but I didn't do that; instead, I found something safe to take my anger out—such as by using a tennis racquet to strike my bed.

Before you can forgive, you need to deal with the harsh emotions that are stirred up by violence. I think of it like this: while I might be angry at a person for punching me or taking my job or cutting me off in my car, my anger is proportionate and, hopefully, so is my response. Many of us feel this way; we are able to handle our emotions and work them through appropriately—our emotions are manageable. However, in the aftermath of violence, the anger reaches such an intensity that it will require much more effort to handle. We may never before have felt this level of anger, and need to learn how to safely discharge it. The first principle, acceptance, goes a long way to diffusing that anger—and may help pave the way for you to forgive—which often is a rational, calm decision, borne of acceptance and the release of anger.

Even if you have not gotten to the place where you can forgive, you can still think about the following elements:

✦ Forgiveness doesn't mean reconciliation with an offender. It in no way suggests that he or she has to know or be part of your thoughts, behavior, or everyday world.
✦ You are not condoning the event in any way, nor do you excuse the loss of your loved one.
✦ If your loved one's death resulted from an action of self-harm (such as suicide, drunk driving, or an overdose), you are not condoning the behavior but, instead, forgiving the person for his or her actions.
✦ You are not pardoning the crime, if there was one. Nor are you forgiving any sentence handed down to a perpetrator. You are not releasing whoever hurt your loved one from responsibility for his or her actions.
✦ You are in no way forgetting what happened; that memory will always be with you and you will find ways of living with it, so that it does not destroy you.

The benefits of forgiveness are many. It enables us to separate whatever violence occurred, from our own self-propelled violent feelings about it. The last thing we want to do is become in any way like whatever harmed our loved one. Yet, if we let it, hate can rule our lives and poison everything we do, ultimately damaging our health and relationships. We wind up making ourselves and everyone around us sick. To forgive is to put an end to that futile form of anger that we have turned without mercy upon ourselves.

There are those who believe that "To err is human; to forgive divine." Perhaps that is the case. We need to work through our anger in order to achieve a transcendent function like forgiveness. In other words, we need to feel the full power of our uglier human emotions upon ourselves, before we can climb to a higher place where we are able to forgive.

Forgiveness also applies to ourselves and those we love. We need to be able to forgive ourselves for what we did or did not do, real or perceived, in the lives of our loved ones. After Aaron died, I began remembering some of the things I had done over the years, such as not always being there for him. I remembered arguments or things I had taken away from him. All of these memories were like knives in my heart. I regretted that I had not been more caring, and hated myself for any unkind word. I consciously, deliberately tortured myself with these things as much as the unbidden "torturers" of my grief did to me. I had to find a way of forgiving myself.

I told Aaron I was sorry for all of the things I did or did not do. I cried and asked for forgiveness. And then I let it go, because I could do no more. It was done. But after I did this, the load felt lighter—I accepted that I could not change anything that happened; I could only forgive myself.

You can do several things: you can ask for forgiveness of the one you lost by writing a letter, or speaking it out loud. You can go to the graveside and ask there. After you do this, it is done. Forgive yourself—and think of the good things, which I am sure are many. Do not allow this to overshadow all the good you shared together.

If your loved one took his or her own life, or lost it as an unintended consequence of some action of which you disapprove, this, too, requires forgiveness, which may be handled in the same was as described above. Isolate the trauma, the damaging act, from the person, and let it go.

Depression and Despair

BEFORE WE MOVE on to gratitude, I want to talk about the feelings of depression and despair, which many of us experience in stage 5.

By the second and third year after Aaron's death, I felt stronger, but my place in the world was still tenuous. It was as though I walked, talked, laughed, but everything had a veil around it. While I continued to try and practice acceptance, I still could not imagine my life fulfilled and happy. Now and then, I would get a glimpse of a new shore and a new world, but it was still too far away. My depression continued. I felt as if I had a heavy stone around me that kept me stuck in the deep. The roads that used to lead to shore were washed out long ago. I couldn't remember who or what I was before. By this time, I think everyone assumed I had gotten over Aaron's death, because I stopped crying all the time. No one ever talked about him. Yet I thought about him almost all the time. It was an unreal feeling to be in the world of the living and at the same time be so preoccupied with the world of the dead.

The second and third years are difficult because you are less likely to talk about your feelings, yet are more likely to feel them. Sharon described it this way:

> The first year, I was just staying alive. The second and third year became much more difficult. I felt depressed even in the middle of something happy. No matter what I did, I had a dead feeling inside. I felt despair when I thought I would have to live like this for the rest of my life. I also thought about suicide, because I didn't want to live that way.

Feelings of depression and despair are a natural response to what you have experienced. They can be dangerous, however, if they persist and take over your life. I encourage you to use your outer network of support to help you with depression, especially if it becomes severe. For example, if symptoms of not eating, sleeping, and thoughts of suicide persist, please talk to a professional about them. Don't give in to the temptation to not talk about your feelings and keep them to yourself. Maybe you are thinking the following:

+ I don't want to bother anybody.
+ Shouldn't I be feeling differently by now?
+ They don't want to hear about my loss anymore.
+ I can't bring myself to tell my story one more time.

I know what these feelings are like. I know, too, that you may have been feeling this quiet grief for so long, you don't remember anything else. It becomes a state of being—one in which you walk, talk, and act as though you're alive, but inside you feel lost or desire to somehow join your loved one. Please know that these are the feelings you need to talk about—the feelings of being abandoned, and the constant immersion in what happened. Talk to a friend, therapist, clergy, or support group. Share how you find this part of the journey so painful—how you just want it to be over. No one will be able to make your despair magically disappear; you still have ahead of you the hard work of suffering. But you may find that, by expressing your feelings, you come out of the isolation—and that in itself will help.

SUICIDAL THOUGHTS

You may experience suicidal thoughts, which, while normal considering the circumstances, must be attended to. I, too, had suicidal feelings because I did not want to live with such ongoing pain. One winter afternoon I had the following thoughts: *I am his mother, and he is lost. So wouldn't I want to find him wherever he is? Wouldn't I go wherever I thought he was, to be with him again?* It seemed perfectly natural to me. And, I couldn't stand the fact that I was always feeling this pain, I wanted it to stop, but it was always there. The only thing was, in order to not feel the pain or to be with my son, it meant that I would have to die, and if I did, my other children would be left alone. I had a dilemma—with whom did I need to be, Aaron, or his brother and sister?

These may sound like crazy thoughts, but they made sense to me, and probably to you, too. However, I was able to understand my thoughts and recognize that's what they were—thoughts. I wasn't going to commit suicide. That said, for some of us, the danger is real. Please do not keep these thoughts to yourself. You must be careful not to become lost in them. Please talk to someone and recognize that, while they are part of your grief, they are fantasies, not actions to be taken.

It is important here to mention post-traumatic stress disorder again because often, depression, suicidal thoughts, and despair accompany symptoms of PTSD. You should be in some form of therapy, as well as using this book, if you find yourself persistently experiencing these symptoms. Ultimately, I cannot emphasize enough the need for you to reach out to someone, whether it is a friend, family, therapist, doctor, clergy, or a support group. I am not saying you should be feeling happy, which may only happen after considerable counseling and care; your goal now is to not feel so *unhappy* as to become physically self-destructive. That is not the road to relief, only to even more pain for yourself and those who love you.

Remember, it will take time to find a life that is meaningful and makes sense. You cannot expect to go through a life-changing trauma such as yours and immediately pick up the pieces and forge ahead, no matter how strong or good your intentions are. Rebuilding a life that has been destroyed takes time, effort, and planning. You need to rebuild from the bottom up. But first we need to find our way out of the deep—and these principles of acceptance, forgiveness, and gratitude will help.

GRATITUDE

Gratitude is a dynamic principle, one that makes us realize what we still have, even after so much has been taken. Gratitude is finding something to be grateful for, no matter how bad the situation is. This is a hard thing to do; people will say to me: "How can I be grateful when such a terrible thing happened?"

I do understand. Yet, surely there is always something to be grateful for. I remember after Aaron died, people used to say to me, "This is the worst thing that could have happened." I thought they were right. Then I realized, no, it wasn't the worst thing that could have happened. Anna and Michael told me something I hadn't known. Once, in the mountains of Evergreen, Colorado, Aaron borrowed the car and was driving with Anna and Michael. The mountain roads had snow on them, as they often do. The kids were having fun, spinning the car in an empty field; Aaron lost control and for a moment they were all frightened. He regained control and they were laughing saying, "Oh God, don't do that. Mom would die if something happened to all three of us."

So, no, it wasn't the worst thing that could have happened. I still had two of my children, and for that I was grateful.

You may not think so, but there is always something more to lose, always something more that can be taken. In our grief, we are naturally focused on what we have lost, rather than what has been spared. The following are words I learned many years ago, and have helped me understand the nature of gratitude:

Give thanks for:
Everything given
Everything taken away
Everything left

"Everything given"

This is a powerful way of looking at things in your life. For example, do you really "own" anything? Perhaps it is more true to say that anything we have is given by grace; while we may work for "things," most of them can be taken away in an instant. This is especially true for the ones we love. We do not own them. They have their own lives and we do not control them. When our children are born, we think of them as "ours." But they do not belong to us; rather they will have a life of their own, and sometimes that life is not what we had planned for them. On the contrary, rarely can it be said that their lives turn out the way we planned. Our children and those we love are gifts given to our care, and we are grateful for the time we have—and what has been given us—precisely because we know it can be taken away at any time. Even though our loved ones have been taken away, we can still be grateful for the time we had with them. This is hard, I know, because it isn't enough; we want them back. Richard said this about his time with Susan:

> After Susan was killed, I didn't care as much about what
> I had with Susan as what I had lost. I wanted her back.
> My children asked me to tell them stories about their
> mother; it made me stop and think about what I did
> have with Susan. The more stories I told about her, the
> more I had. It didn't change the fact I missed her, but it
> did make me grateful for what I did have with her.

"Everything taken"

Gratitude is being thankful not only for what was given, but what has been taken, too. At first, this sounds really odd. Why would you be grateful for what has been taken? Surely that goes against everything we know and feel. But think about it—even though someone has been taken, weren't they first given to you? In other words, you cannot lose something or someone you once had. All those moments are still there, within you, in memories perhaps as fresh as the reality when they were forged. Therefore, you did at one time have the joy of that person, and for that you can be grateful. Very often, the thing that brings us pain is the thing that once brought us joy. Would you have refused the gift of love from someone simply because it bears the risk of being taken away?

No, we accept the gift of love, knowing that sometimes it will bring us great suffering. And sometimes, it is that very suffering that makes us love more. So when you think of what has been taken away, try to keep in mind that there is another side of the coin: gratitude that what we loved had existed at all.

"Everything left"

This may be the greatest gift of gratitude: Not everything has been taken from us. It never is. There is always something left behind to be grateful for—the task is to find it.

After Aaron died, I found a little wooden box into which I had put some things several years before. When I opened it, I found a pin that Aaron had given me when he was eight or nine years old. I remembered he was so excited to give it me—it was a funny kind of bird with two little green stones for eyes and a shiny yellow stone for a tail. I remember loving it because he gave it to me, but laughing because it was so funny looking. When I saw it this time, it became the most beautiful thing I could imagine, because it was something I had that he had touched and given to me. I was so grateful for this funny little bird, it was left for me to treasure, after so much had been taken.

To develop gratitude in your life, make a list answering the following questions. The answers can be short and can relate to your immediate circumstances:

+ What has been given to you?
+ What has been taken away?
+ And what is left for you to love and be grateful for?

Acknowledge your pain and your suffering for what has been taken, but examine, too, what has been left. See how precious it now becomes? There is always something to be grateful for, if only we will look. Gratitude is a dynamic principle, because it causes something good to happen. Violence has obviously brought painful changes and has taken good out of your life, whereas gratitude brings something back. It causes you to recognize there is something left in your life to start over with.

Without gratitude, we feel continually bereft and stuck in our loss. There is no way out. Gratitude is like the gentle wave that brings something to nourish you while you are treading water. It gives you something to look forward to, something that will help you find your way to the other shore.

The Coral Reef

GENERATING CREATIVITY

AFTER WE HAVE lost someone to violence, many of us they feel as though we, too, have died. As Valerie said,

> When Devon was killed by that stray bullet, it hit me, too. He was my child, my life. I felt dead, like nothing would grow inside me again. Death brings awful feelings with it—sharing in that death, feeling barren and walking in the desert—that's what I felt, especially in the early years after he died.

Violence cuts us to our roots; we feel that nothing will grow again—the damage has been so deep. That is why so often in the first years after our trauma, we seem aimless, wandering, disconnected from life, because the notion of death and dying colors so much of what we think and do. We feel severed from the human root of creativity. The natural impulse to create becomes the struggle to survive. Creativity must prevail—otherwise we remain caught in the destructive act of violence over and over again. We stay in the deep and we cannot find our way out.

Stage 6 shows us a way out of the deep. A coral reef is an intricate living wall found in the ocean. It teems with life, abounding with all sorts of marvelous sea animals, fanciful creations, and lovely strange things, not seen above water; in fact, you must be in the water to see the reef, often diving to great depths.

You can create your own coral reef out of the depths of your sorrow and suffering. Let creativity become the living, breathing expression of your ongoing struggle with the destructive aspects of violence. For you, the coral reef represents the beautiful regenerative quality of life and overcoming a violent death. To generate is to grow something. Your very recognition of this is a statement that you will not be destroyed but, instead, will create and grow—you will live again.

You may feel you cannot grow again, so deep is the cut, but you can and you will; the imperative of life is that it goes on—in one form or another. Embracing your creativity is a crucial, pivotal stage in your journey, and one that must be undertaken. This chapter will guide you on this essential part of your journey and will explore the following:

+ What is creativity?
+ Imagine being creative.
+ Mediums of creativity:
  + Storytelling
  + Scrapbooking
  + Writing
  + Painting, drawing, collage
  + Needlework
  + Mask making
  + Working with clay
  + Music
  + Dance
  + Gardening

+ Nature
+ Other ways to be creative
+ Memorials and gravesites
+ Anniversaries, holidays, birthdays
+ Community organizations and memorials
+ A creative life

Don't worry if you think you are not "the creative type"—this is not a display of who's got the greatest talent—quite the contrary. It's simply presenting ways to help you get in touch with your creativity and your own expression of it. Please keep in mind that the purpose here is to counter the violent, destructive force of death with the vital creative, living energy of life—something we all need to invite back into our own lives.

First, you will explore the notion of creativity and then move on to an exercise. After you have done the exercise, read through the mediums that follow—you may be surprised by which ones appeal to you. You may already have creative projects in mind, and this may be the incentive to help you move forward to beginning them.

What Is Creativity?

THIS IS ONE of the greatest gifts we possess as human beings. Our greatest works of art, literature, film, and music come directly out of our human experience. Our acts of heroism, goodness, and sacrifice often come directly out of our suffering. Creativity is an act of life in response to the chaos of violence.

We are, by the very nature of our humanity, creative; it is the energy of life itself. While some people may find themselves thinking, "I'm not creative," this attitude actually denies a crucial part of humanity. All living beings possess creative energy; the question is, what do we do with it?

For some men, this energy is often looked upon as "women's territory." Yet, many celebrated artists, musicians, architects, choreographers . . . are men. Creativity is not gender specific; so while scrapbooking, for example, may not appeal to some men, there are many other unique ways for you to express this energy.

After we lose someone to violence, the last thing we may feel like doing is creating something new, giving life to anything—whether that be an idea, a garden, or a photograph. This stage of the journey seeks to help you recover the energy of life—the essence of creativity. No matter how you express it, the important thing is to do it.

Imagine Being Creative

HERE'S AN EXERCISE to help you open yourself to your creative energy, no matter which stage you are in. I do need to say that, in the very early stages of grief, it may be difficult to anchor this exercise. Many people report that it is harder to stay focused during that period, because the waves of grief are so difficult to manage. However, if you feel up to it, please do try the exercise—you may be surprised by where it takes you.

First, make sure you have about fifteen to thirty minutes of uninterrupted time. Choose a quiet place where you won't be bothered. Now get comfortable, sitting up, rather than lying down (you might fall asleep if you are lying down!). Place your feet on the floor and your hands in your lap.

Read this following visualization to yourself three times. Slowly. Then allow yourself to imagine what you remember from reading. Let's start:

First, take a nice deep breath. Relax your shoulders. Relax your neck.

Try some shoulder and neck rolls—slowly and carefully move your head in a circular motion, toward your chest. Then roll your shoulders, moving them up toward your head and then in a circular motion. Continue a nice steady breath and again, relax your shoulders and neck. Imagine your body calming down, relaxing, and tell yourself that your tensions can leave with your outgoing breath.

With each breath, feel yourself relaxing even more. Picture tension floating above your head and out from your toes, onto the floor below them.

Settle in; listen to your breath, which is like a breeze blowing through your mind. Soft, quiet, at rest.

Imagine yourself in the ocean, floating. Do not be afraid. You will not drown. Today the ocean is calm, quiet—in fact, you know this place; it has been your home for a while now.

As you look, an object becomes clear to you. It is a lovely, breathing wall of coral. You see that it is full of life, with fish and soft billowy creatures of all colors and shapes and sizes; it is a wonderland of life and it makes you feel alive.

You are enthralled by its beauty and fascinated with its movement—you have never seen anything like it except perhaps in a dream. The colors of coral and the creatures that live on it are blue, green, pink, red, gold. You are mesmerized by its beauty.

You feel this aliveness deep inside and realize this wall is a part of you—perhaps forgotten, but it still lives inside. Despite everything. You have found it within. It inspires and stirs your energy.

You realize this is your life and there is a rich place of creativity within.

Imagine yourself in front of your reef, adding things to the wall, changing things around as you wish and making the image your own, in whatever way you choose.

Realize this is the image you will keep with you, one to which you can return at any time. It is yours; you can do what you want with it.

When you are ready to leave, come out of the visualization, take a nice deep breath, and either take a break or read on.

This exercise will help generate creativity within. It will help you when you are feeling tense and inspire you to acknowledge your own coral reef and work with it as an ongoing image.

Creative Mediums

STORYTELLING

You began your journey in stage 1, with telling your story. At that time, it was important to shape it into something you could carry, without it crushing you. At that time you were more concerned with your actual ability to tell hard facts, than with imbuing the story with creativity.

Your story at that time had more to do with the violent act that changed everything. What you will be doing now is telling more than that. You will now want to include the life of the one you loved—and your life, too.

This is how Sharon described it:

> For a long time, I could only tell the story of how Jack was murdered—and the grief consumed me. Later, I clung to memories of how it was between us, but it seemed like it was either/or. Then I began to think of ways I could make his life the important story and the murder a part, but not all, of it.

Because our focus is creativity, I will ask you to think about ways you can tell your story with life, rather than death, as the central theme. For example, you can start with yourself. Tell yourself a story about something your loved one did—like the following story Sharon tells:

> Jack loved to play golf; I remember how excited he would be when we went on vacation and he had a new course to play. I used to laugh, because that would be the time he seemed so much younger, like a young boy—he'd put on a new hat from the course and with a big grin, he'd head out—I liked to see him enjoy himself that way.

Think of a story of your loved one and how good you felt then. Perhaps it's a funny moment, or a memory of something your loved one liked to do, a hobby, an activity, or something the person did for you or someone else. Use Sharon's story above as a guide; it can be a simple moment of pleasure you had with your loved one. It doesn't have to have deep significance, but merely reflect a happier time.

The purpose of this new storytelling is to place emphasis on the life of the person and to then include it on occasions when you talk about what happened. It is a way of forcing the violence to let go of its grip and command of the story, and let the life of your loved one be told as well.

You can also tell stories with your family. As an exercise, try gathering together with the purpose of each telling a story about the life—not death—of your loved one. My family once got together and told the story of how, on a car trip from California to Colorado, we stopped at a hotel, exhausted and cranky. Aaron, who was fourteen at the time, jumped on the beds and pretended he was a dinosaur, chasing everyone and shrieking like a raptor. We all fell to the floor laughing. When we told the story, we remembered what a comic Aaron was and how he had a knack for turning things into something funny. In this telling, we overcame the violent act by a testimony of his life. You can do the same—it seems like a small thing, but the sum of many small things is strong enough to turn the tide of sorrow.

The purpose here is to remember life, and yes, it will be sad, and yes, it will be hard, but your story will also have a creative, alive quality that no act of violence can take away.

Telling these kinds of stories will get you ready to use them in creative mediums. You can choose the ones that follow or create your own. Don't be afraid to try new forms—your coral reef can have many different and wonderful shapes and colors, all living and breathing forms of life.

SCRAPBOOKING

Scrapbooking has become one of the most popular creative mediums for storytelling. It is simply a concept of gathering together the pictures of your loved one and placing them in a book, with unlimited creative touches. These touches will be your unique personal expression. This book becomes a beautiful record of your story. It can include mementos, pictures, writings, anything you wish.

Linda said the following:

> I had so many things of Sam's. Even though he was only ten, he had awards from school, Little League, and all kinds of stuff. I chose a beautiful scrapbook, and put in his awards, and pictures of him with his Boy Scout pins. It became a project for me, one which I cried over and sometimes couldn't go near, but I love it, just like I loved him; it's full of memories of happy things.

If you choose to use this medium, you will want to get a scrapbook that you like. There are many to choose from and they can be found at specialty stores, drugstores, and department stores. Choose one that has significance for you. For example, it could the favorite color of your loved one. For Linda it was yellow, Sam's favorite color. The cover of your scrapbook could also be a scene of something you like or one that reminds you of a place that was special to your loved one. Sharon chose a cover of a deep green field, like a golf course.

Before you begin the actual creation of your scrapbook, get organized by assembling a collection of photos, letters, and other things that are reminders of the person, along with whatever else you may want to incorporate.

You may also want to put together a "tool box" for your supplies—things like glue, scissors, photo corners, etc., which will make it easier for you to keep track of where your tools are.

Many crafts and women's magazines and online resources can assist you in your scrapbooking. You can even find groups in your area that offer support, instruction, and help. Look at the resources in the appendix for more information.

Next, you will want to gather your pictures and mementos, and decide which ones will go into your book. This will be a bittersweet experience. You will probably cry, feel angry, and stop and restart your project. Nonetheless, you will have a beautiful story when you are finished. It will tell about the life of the one you love. It will be something that the next generation will treasure.

You can also ask family members and friends to contribute to the scrapbook, whether by writing a memory of the person or giving you something they wish to put into the book, thereby creating a group memorial—one which will honor your loved one and create an archive—one that you can continue to add to.

WRITING

While you may have written your story in stage 1, I'm talking about a more creative form here. For example, in writing your story more creatively, you can tell not only what happened, but who your loved one was and what your family relationship or friendship with him or her was like. You can include whatever you wish in your story. If you are already writing in a journal, you may want to continue to give your story life in that format. You can add decorations, or add poetry, or any other embellishments to your journal.

You can also create a "memory book." To begin, either use the journal you have been writing in or choose one for this project. Begin by writing about a memory of your loved one. In this book, you have read many examples of memories survivors have shared about their loved ones. Here's another example of one of mine:

Aaron was about five at the time. We lived in a row home in Philadelphia. At the corner of our street, there was a store that sold candy. One evening, he came to me in his pajamas and said, "Mom, let's get some candy at the store."

I said, "Aaron, we're in our pj's and it's dark outside; I don't want to get dressed."

In his sweet little way, he said, "Mom, let's just put our coats on and get some!"

So we did—we put our coats over our pajamas and went to the store, bought some candy, and came back and ate it, laughing.

I remember this because I was always so busy, I wasn't very spontaneous, but this time I was and that memory of us with our coats over our pajamas will always be precious to me.

We may not realize it immediately, but there is one thing that death and violence cannot take away from us: our memories. I didn't realize this until a few months after Aaron's death. The memories I had of him would always be mine. They existed before the murder; they were untouched by the violence. They were the jewels I took out in times of grief and held close to me—they helped me when sometimes nothing else would. In documenting these memories, each one of us can honor our loved ones. Once they are set down on paper, they truly live on, they can be seen and touched and read aloud, far beyond their intangible home in our minds and hearts.

The medium of writing may be used in other forms as well. You can write a letter telling people how you are and what you want them to know; perhaps you may decide to include a story or a memory, or pictures of your loved one. This letter can be sent out to your extended family and friends, people whom you care about but don't speak to often. Many people live far away and you may not be able to visit them. Sometimes it is exhausting to call everyone on the phone, but sending a letter is a fine way to communicate, again giving them more to hold on to than a conversation that was far more ephemeral.

If you want to begin writing but are having difficulty, try the following "free-form" exercise, which will help you open up and express your story in different ways:

Sit quietly with pen and paper in hand, or before your journal or your computer. Tell yourself you are going to write a few lines about how you feel. Close your eyes and breathe slowly and evenly, in and out, taking five deep breaths. Think of yourself on the beach, looking at the sky, or even the ocean you just came out of. Now think of a story that you want to tell—a memory or a thought or how you feel.

Now write it down—don't worry about what it looks or sounds like. When you are done, look at what you have written and thank yourself for writing it.

Now decide how you want to shape it, whether it is for your memory book, scrapbook, letter, or journal.

Some enjoy writing poetry and others would like to but don't know how. Historically, poetry has been used to express many emotions—love, longing, fear, to name a few. It is also used for elegies, and many people find solace in expressing their thoughts through the poetic form.

Although you may feel intimidated, please do not be afraid to write your own poetry. You can reach inside and find words to convey your deepest feelings and emotions. If you want to write a poem, try the following exercise:

Draw a circle in the middle of a piece of paper. Write a word inside the circle that represents your loved one. Then take five minutes and write other words in the circle, that relate to the first word. For example, I wrote "Aaron" in the middle of my circle and then drew arrows to other words, such as love, son, gift, light, sweet. Choose your own and try to keep some of them joyful or happy.

Then write a poem using the words, adding more if you wish. Here's mine:

> Aaron, you are love
> A gift of life
> My son, my light
> My sweet smile,
> Always with me

After you have written a few lines, go back and shape it; it doesn't have to rhyme; it only has to say what you feel. The above poem is simple, yet heartfelt. It conveys what I feel—and that's all you have to do.

PAINTING, DRAWING, COLLAGE

Remember your art classes in elementary school? While you may not be "artistic," still you may remember the pleasure you experienced while finger-painting or crayoning, if only in the distant past. Painting, drawing, and collage can be wonderful creative mediums to tell your story.

It can be as simple as getting inexpensive paper and some paints—oil, watercolor, acrylic. Other mediums include pastels, charcoal, graphite and colored pencils, and colored inks . . . or even crayons or finger-paints. You can go to any art store or retailer that sells supplies and select the materials you wish, depending on how serious you want to get about your painting or drawing.

Here's a story from Tara, whose sister, Vicki, was killed:

> I liked art and did some painting in high school. When Vicki was killed, I got out my old supplies and painted big red and black abstracts, because I was so angry. Later, I also painted beautiful green and pink ones, too. What I found was it helped my moods. I just painted whatever I felt like. I wasn't interested in whether they were "good" art.

Tara's experience tells us the therapeutic benefits of art are many. She was creating directly out of her feelings, and, as a result, unleashed some deep emotions that she could recognize and deal with. You can do the same. If you wish, you can even utilize art as a therapeutic approach to healing, which I mentioned in stage 3, and find an art therapist to work with.

Although you may just want to draw or paint on your own, you might want to take classes. You can find them in art schools, community centers, and in the adult education division at your local Y. Nan, the woman who came to me before Aaron died, painted beautiful flowers that reminded her of her daughter. This was Nan's answer to violence, creating new life through her painting. She became an accomplished painter, and her work has been displayed at many galleries.

Brenda, on the other hand, just wanted to draw without extra instruction:

> I always loved to draw when I was young, then I climbed the corporate ladder and forgot about it. After my daughter Ellie was killed, I quit my job; I began drawing, first just to doodle, and then, something shifted. I began enjoying my time drawing—I wanted to make it more a part of my life. I needed this creativity to feel alive—it helped me remember a better time in my life, when I was young and happy.

Collage is an interesting way to piece together parts of your story through pictures and symbols. For example, in graduate school I wanted to express the idea of the influences of my life, during an art therapy class. I gathered some photos but also used many different symbols, such as the mountains of Italy or the Celtic knot, and placed them on a piece of art board—so they were connected, therefore creating a collage. It gave the feeling of all of these influences being a part of one another, not separate pieces.

You can make a collage by purchasing a piece of art board, which is available in most art supply stores. It can be rigid or not, depending on what effect you want. Then gather the photos or other paper items you want to use, perhaps looking through magazines, catalogs, and art books for the pictures you want to add. Sharon, for instance, used a picture of a golf course for her collage of her husband. She called the finished piece "Jack's Favorite Things."

These expressions of creative energy can be healing, insightful, and bring you pleasure. Be adventurous!

NEEDLEWORK

You may find needlework very relaxing. There are many forms you can choose: quilting, embroidery, knitting, or making samplers with your favorite patterns or sayings.

Mary made a quilt from the doll clothes her daughter, Amy, had when she was a young child; in the center of the quilt, she placed Amy's picture and embroidered her favorite poem.

Iris, who was living in New York City when the 9/11 attacks occurred, told me the following:

> After 9/11 I knitted like a fiend; that Christmas seven friends got scarves, and one a shawl . . . all quite complex patterns, which I'd had to concentrate on; aside from working out my agitation, it was also a means of demonstrating my feelings of renewed closeness toward and appreciation for all the—thankfully safe—recipients.

MASK MAKING

Mask making is a craft and therapeutic technique used to help us see the masks we wear in life that we show to other people.

Often, in grief, we will wear a mask so that people will not see our suffering. Sometimes, we pretend that things are all right when, underneath the mask, we are crying, in pain, unable to reach out. We may think we cannot take these masks off, and may indeed not know how to take them off and show others how we feel.

Mask making can be a powerful experience. The process can help you take off the mask of your facial expression and manner, and be more authentic to yourself and others. Andrea, who experienced mask making, said,

> After Ryan committed suicide, I wore a mask of frozen feelings. I couldn't show people how I felt, the shame I felt about not saving my son. I couldn't face it in myself,

so I couldn't let other people see it. I took the mask-making workshop and made a mask that was the one I showed people—the frozen me. The facilitator had me put it on so people could tell me what they saw: a person whose feelings were shut off, not alive. I wanted to keep it on because it felt safe, but I knew it was keeping me stuck. The facilitator helped me take it off. Once I did, I felt naked and vulnerable; I cried—but I looked around and people reached out their hands to me. I let them see what I was really feeling.

Mask making can help you both recognize and take off your mask. There are mask-making workshops, which will help direct your experience (resources are listed in the appendix), but you can also make your own mask. Do this by getting a plain face mask at an art store. Assemble paints, brushes, and things you might want to add, such as feathers or beads. If you prefer, you can make it quite plain. Begin by painting the mask as you see yourself. Are you pretending you're okay, frozen, numb, sad? Let your imagination be your guide and paint your mask as you see yourself.

Recognize that, often, the mask you wear in your everyday life to hide your real feelings from others will keep you from sharing yourself with those that can help you. Practice putting on and then taking off the mask you have created before a mirror, to allow yourself to see what's underneath. Try and accept yourself for what you are experiencing. See your grief for what it is: a part, but not all, of you. Your mask is an expression of your reaction to the violence, but it is not who you are.

WORKING WITH CLAY

Years ago, before I started graduate school, I noticed that the community center down the road was offering a sculpting class. I knew nothing about sculpting but signed up for the class anyway. It was in a lovely, sunny studio in California. On the first day, I choose a big lump of clay and started molding it into . . . what, I wasn't sure.

The clay began to take the shape of a figure. A girl emerged; she looked Egyptian. I was excited. I worked and worked, and, with the help of my wonderful teacher, out came the figure of a young girl with an Egyptian headdress and arms joined at her waist. I had used a metal pole to build her on; when the sculpture was done, my teacher and I attempted to lift her off. As we lifted her, the top of my girl went flying! When I reshaped her, she had a whole new body—one I guess she wanted.

The statue of the girl was a guide through graduate school, signaling the beginning of a long journey. I never took another sculpture class, nor did I make another statue, but I still have her with me as a reminder of that time in my life.

You can make something, too, whether it is a statue or any other object you choose. Working with your hands and creating something out of the raw material of clay can be a rewarding and enlivening experience. After all, doesn't clay come directly from the earth—a symbol of where we all return in one form or another? Shaping something out of it is a testimony to the remarkable ability of the earth to produce something again, even after death.

MUSIC

One of the most enduring gifts humans give to one another is music. It is the sound of joy, sadness, inspiration, and love. It makes us reach out to one another. It "soothes the savage breast" and helps us become more in tune with life—with all its beauty and its sadness.

You can put your favorite music on or go to a live performance, and allow it to enliven you and stir your creative juices and energy. You can also play music with others. There are many forms this can take. You might wish to take a music class and learn an instrument, or to return to an instrument that you used to play. Some instruments are quite easy to learn—and some, like the tambourine and maracas, are so simple you just need to shake them.

You can also sing. Your singing doesn't have to be of professional quality. Sometimes it feels wonderful to simply belt out tunes in the shower or along with the radio. If you feel you want to share your voice, you may want to join a choir or a community chorus, and sing, sing, sing.

DANCE

Dancing is a wonderful form of creativity. It moves our bodies to express the gamut of emotions and human experience. We have dances of joy, sorrow, victory, and grief. Rent a video or go to a performance of modern, folk, jazz, and ballet dance, or any number of ethnic dance styles. While watching, allow yourself to be moved by the passion and performance of the dancers, and for a moment to be lifted from your own sorrow into the creative life. And you can dance, too, whether it is by taking classes or just going out dancing. When you hear music that makes you want to move, you can find yourself simply letting go, letting your body move, having fun.

Sheila, who had lost both her daughter and grandson, became an accomplished ballroom dancer at age seventy-three! She said,

> I always wanted to dance when I was younger, but never did. And of course, when Gina and Larry died, I didn't want to dance at all. But four years later, I decided to give it a try and I feel so alive. I love it; it is one of the things I really enjoy. Now, I dance through life, the good and the bad, one day at a time.

GARDENING

Gardening is a nurturing act of creativity. You till the soil, preparing it so that it receives the seed. You choose lovely colors and shapes and sizes of things you want to plant. You put your hands in the rich soil and nurture your seedlings until they grow into their full beauty.

And, if you wish, you can plant gardens in the name of your loved one, and marvel with joy when you see the flowers in bloom.

On the Mother's Day before Aaron died, I planted flowers in the small garden in front of my new house. I am sorry to say that very few of them survived, which seemed fitting, considering what else was going on. Yet ever since, I have planted flowers every Memorial Day, and I love to see them bloom. It reminds me that life can flower again—out of the same ground in which we might bury our loved ones—and we keep trying, hoping that, this year, they will bloom.

If you like to garden or would like to try, think of your patch of earth as a place where life can begin again. Pick things that will grow according to your soil and weather (ask for help at your local nursery or gardening center, or consult seed catalogs for the correct zones), so you won't become frustrated and disappointed if an inappropriate plant fails to thrive. Plant flowers that are important to you and those that you remember your loved one cared for. Include some new ones, to add variety and promise of change.

Take time to enjoy your garden and the renewing power of life. Sit in your garden and write, meditate, or dream. Keep it as your own special, private place or ask your family to join you there to share memories and tell stories of your loved one. If you do not have a garden, a window box or indoor planter could still support beautiful life forms. Quite a number of flowering plants will bloom indoors, with proper conditions and care.

There are also many beautiful community gardens for your enjoyment. You can visit and draw in the loveliness and be inspired by the regenerative power of beauty, and perhaps you might wish to inquire if you may volunteer to help tend the plants.

Some people have planted memorial gardens to honor their loved ones. I know of at least one park that members of Parents of Murdered Children planted, here in Pennsylvania. This park is an excellent example of how we can employ our creative energy and take back our lives from the violence that has permeated them. This garden and others like it are important reminders that, while violence destroys life, it will not have the last word. We who survive will plant again and life will grow.

NATURE

Surely nature is the greatest source of art there is. We can enjoy it no matter what the season or the terrain. There is stunning beauty in the dry desert as well as in the moist tropical jungles. These extremes are simply different expressions of life.

Do not pass up the tremendous gift of nature. It is one of the most powerful ways to regenerate your broken life. You can enjoy nature in many ways: hiking, camping, or just driving to or through a beautiful vista. Or you can decide to spend some time away where you can find peace, quiet, and a view. There are many resources available for this. You can rent a cabin in the woods or up in the mountains, or rent an apartment in the countryside; maybe someone you know already has a getaway you can use. You may prefer to go to the seashore; when you see the stretch of ocean in front of you, you can imagine your journey and how far you have come.

If you cannot travel, then take advantage of your local city parks, gardens, or nature preserves. Wherever you find it, remember that nature is the oldest example of creativity and renewal in everyday life. As nature's cycles shift from death to rebirth, so do our own lives.

OTHER WAYS TO BE CREATIVE

Building
Often, when people rebuild their homes after a fire or disaster, they have a sense of triumph. They feel they have persevered and overcome destruction—they defy it and rebuild and live again.

After Aaron died, his fraternity, the Prodigal Sons, built a wooden box for me, with his name engraved on it. Inside were letters of love they had written for Aaron, along with Aaron's T-shirt from the fraternity. I love looking at the box and count it among my most precious possessions.

You can build something, whether it is a display case for your loved one's belongings, a new room to do new things in, or any of the things that build up, rather than tear down; create, rather than destroy.

Collections

People collect all kinds of different objects. You might have a collection of baseball cards or plates or coins or really anything that is valuable to you. This is also where many men find their creativity. Richard, who lost this wife, Susan, said,

> Well, I am not interested in painting or anything like that, but I have a collection of coins. I started with my father years ago. When Susan died, I started to become interested in them again and found myself looking forward to collecting them, and reading their history. I felt interested in something again and that was good for me.

Gary said the following after his son was killed in Iraq:

> James had a collection of awards and ribbons he had gotten through the years, and also all of his military stuff. After he died, I built a showcase for everything he had. It was really a good display, I put so much feeling and caring into it, and it made me feel good to use my hands and build something for him.

Sports

Sports can be challenging and rewarding; they can be an excellent way of expressing creativity. Any sport you play will help you; the one caveat is to watch out for competitiveness. While, of course, you want to win, the idea here is to play and allow your creative juices to flow, rather than to use the sport as an exercise in aggression. In fact, try to play a few games just for fun and see what happens.

Play

Let's not forget one of the best forms of creativity ever—play. If you watch young children play, you will see creativity in action—wonderful, happy, silly, and spontaneous play. Remember when you were a kid and played games, such as hide-and-seek or tag? Do you remember the last time you played? What was it like? Perhaps you can write down the story. Has it been a long time? If it has, it's time to play again, so get out your pencil, paint, clay, music, or any other form you can think of, or join some children at play (or teach *them* the games you enjoyed as a child—hopscotch, say, or jump-rope), and let go—just play for a while.

Holidays, Birthdays, and Anniversaries

STAGE 4 ACKNOWLEDGED the challenges of the first year of holidays, birthdays, and the anniversary of your loved one's death. At that stage, we were specifically concerned with getting through the first year. Stage 6 addresses how to bring creativity back into these significant dates. You may have been able to do this even in the first year; however, many people report that their first year was so agonizing and they were in such shock, they couldn't even deal with the dates. Sharon tells the following story:

> I barely remember the first year of holidays; I think I just white-knuckled it and muddled through. Much of what I did was for my children, so they might have some sense of the holiday, but I think they, too, were in shock, and we all just passed the time. It was such a relief when it was over.

Holidays are, of course, times when people celebrate the happiness and joy of the season. For those who have experienced a profound loss, those joys are eclipsed by that loss. Yet, as time goes on, you can create new ways to celebrate the holidays without feeling as if you are somehow being disrespectful or unfaithful to your loved one's memory. There are ways you can help yourself to bring light into your life again, by creating new traditions as well as honoring the old ones. Your loved one can be made a part of your observances, in whatever creative way you can.

You might wish to purchase something new that will represent your loved one.

Ron told me that, on the third Hanukkah after Debra's death, he purchased a new menorah. He had her name engraved, and the diamond from her wedding ring placed near her name. When his children light the candles, they are all reminded of her presence and of their commitment of love for each other. This gives Ron some peace—and a way he can celebrate the holiday.

Many of us will have traditions we will want to honor and continue to observe. Rita always made a special pie for Don on Thanksgiving; after his death, she decided to continue making it in his honor. Everyone in the family looked forward to eating it, remembering Don and how much he enjoyed it.

At Christmas in our house, I give my children presents from their father, who passed away, and now from Aaron, too. I write on the gifts, "To Anna from Aaron" or "To Mike from Aaron." This is a way of keeping their father and brother alive and in our lives, and always part of our holidays.

You can also reach out to others in the name of your loved one. One way would be to volunteer at a soup kitchen; another, by helping a needy family or an underprivileged child by providing food and clothing, or by giving to others, such as a hospital's children's ward or a senior citizen center, the gifts you would have given your loved one. There are many, many ways to give from your heart to someone who needs your help. Perhaps this is a truly creative way to say that good can overcome violence.

Celebrating birthdays challenges you because the paradox, of course, is that you should be celebrating another year of life with the one you love. But how do you cope now? What can you do to honor your loved one and not feel devastated by the person's absence?

August 14, 2005, would have been Aaron's twenty-seventh birthday. I went to the cemetery with two small rose bushes, a red one from my mother, and a yellow one from me. It was a hot day, high nineties, reminding me of the day we buried him.

The ground was hard from the hot and dry weather, but I dug a hole and I planted the bushes as best I could. I poured water over them, wondering if they would survive. As I dug, I wondered what would happen if I kept digging. Would I hit his coffin? The old grief came again, with the indescribable sadness and pain. I felt like digging until I reached him: maybe I could wake him up, and maybe I would just climb in the hole and stay there. As much as I was tempted to do this, instead, I stretched out on the ground and listened to the breeze rustling through the huge tree overhead. I saw the clouds above in the clear blue sky and felt Aaron's spirit floating above the horizon.

Later that night, I couldn't sleep. I saw lights flashing behind the blinds and heard thunder crack the sky. Then the rain started, and I heard it falling, strong and sure. I felt relief; the roses wouldn't die, at least not tonight. Life-giving rain would save them—and, for the moment, me.

Think of ways you can bring new life into the birthday of your loved one. You may wish to plant flowers or give a donation in his or her name. You may volunteer in some capacity, or do someone a special service, such as by giving someone else a birthday party who wouldn't have one otherwise. Whatever you do, do it in a way that is life-affirming.

The anniversary of the death can be the most challenging date of all. This is the day that divided your life into what was and what is now. Regardless of how strong you feel and all the steps you are taking to celebrate life, this is an awful day. Yet, perhaps this is the day that you need to bring life into most, because this is the day when it was taken away. I will tell you that I still cannot bear Memorial Day. The whole month is just so difficult. Yet, I can tell you that my grief has changed through the years, and I am sure it will continue to change.

Many survivors will pass the day in quiet ways or, perhaps, do something for another. I believe that, sometimes, just getting through it is the most creative act.

However you can, bring your own creativity to these special times of the year. Remember, too, that each year, they will be different, because time will change you—and hopefully each year will bring new life and new occasions for celebration.

Things They Used to Own

OUR LOVED ONES leave behind many material possessions, some more than others. Often, the question of what to do with these things is painful. Deciding what to do with your loved one's things—the stuff of his or her life, what possessions were important to the person—is no easy task and often presents a dilemma. These items are precious to us and it is a challenge to even start to tackle this. However, at some point, you need to think openly about the belongings of the person you loved.

Aaron had very few things. We were not living in the house he grew up in; therefore, I didn't have "his room" to think about. He was a college student and had few belongings, other than clothes and a few mementos. The first year, I could hardly go through the boxes. It was just too painful, and I had no idea what to do with these items. After a year had passed, I gathered the strength to go through them more thoroughly. I gave away his clothes to people who would wear them; it helped to know his clothes kept someone warm. Aaron had a red cap he was famous for wearing; it found a new home with his brother, Mike. I kept all of his other things and put them with his childhood awards.

Andrea, who lost her son, Ryan, gave his clothes to a charitable organization, but kept his collection of baseball cards in a special case. Jennifer had a special box made, in which she could keep her sister's jewelry.

You may have more or fewer belongings to sort through. You may choose to keep a child's or other relation's room or personal spaces completely as it was, or add other things as time goes on.

You must decide, in your own time, what you will do with particular items. It will sometimes feel overwhelming, the most ordinary objects suddenly taking on enormous significance. Cry when you need to, but remember, too, these things are so precious. Don't be hasty, and don't let others force upon you what decisions you need to make for yourself. Ask yourself how you can best use the items to preserve the memory of the one to whom they belonged.

Keep the smallest things sacred and choose a lovely box or container for them. They will be your special secret—the thing you take out when you need to know your loved one is still close to you.

Gravesites

THIS IS A topic not many of us want to talk about, let alone think of "creatively." Yet, this is the place where, for many of us, our loved ones will rest. In the case of cremation, there will be an urn or the ashes will be scattered. In some instances, unfortunately, there will not be a body to bury.

If you are burying your loved one, you will most likely choose a memorial stone to be placed at the head of the grave. In the Jewish tradition, the stone at the grave marks where the person passed through in this world. These markers tell us that the person was here in this life, and has left his or her body for us to honor. Many times, the marker is not placed at the grave until the following year, giving you time to choose the inscription you will use. The inscription doesn't have to be just birth and death dates; you may wish to choose a quotation or something else significant for the one you love.

For example, I chose a Celtic cross, with wild roses to symbolize our ancestry and the wild roses I had always loved—and the wild rose bush Aaron and Brian's bodies were found under. Lisa chose lilies for her mother's headstone, because her mother had always loved them, especially at Easter. Mary chose a trumpet vine for

Amy. Select symbols that are both appropriate for their place and meaningful to you. You can ask the memorial creator for help, and he or she will try to accommodate your wishes.

The cemetery is a place many may wish to visit and honor. Yet, everyone will have a different relationship with the gravesite; likewise, one may not feel the same way about a grave, year in and year out. For me, sometimes I can visit Aaron's grave and other times, I cannot. In the first year, I dreaded even the thought of it. Then I would feel tremendous guilt for not visiting him. I felt so chaotic; I just couldn't handle it most of the time. Paula, on the other hand, was able to visit her son's grave very often. In fact, she would decorate Peter's grave for each holiday. It was beautiful. She would bring special things that had meaning, and would gain tremendous comfort from this. I admired that and it helped me see how I could do that for Aaron.

Cultures throughout the world have ways of honoring the dead, especially at the gravesite. What comes to mind is el Dia de Los Muertos, or Day of the Dead, celebrated in Mexico. On November 1, people go to the gravesites of their loved ones, especially the graves of little children, who are called the little angels. On November 2, favorite foods and special flowers are brought for the adults who are deceased. Relatives and friends stay for the day, honoring their loved ones, eating and drinking with them and celebrating their lives.

If you have chosen cremation, you may want to select a special box or an urn for the ashes, or may choose instead to sprinkle the ashes in a special place. This can be a beautiful, creative act. Whatever you decide, you will want to respect the wishes of your loved one while also incorporating some of your own ideas. Rita explained,

> Don did not want to be buried, I knew that. I wanted to honor his wishes and have him cremated. I knew his favorite place was a hill overlooking a river. We used to go there all the time. Derek, his brother, and I went there early one morning, and we both said our good-bye's and scattered Don's ashes. I often go there

now, and this spot always recalls the good times. I feel him close by.

If you do not have the body of your loved one, there are still things you can do to both honor him or her and to make a special "memorial" place for yourself and your family or friends. Whether or not there is a body, you can create a memorial or a funeral service to say farewell. Speak to your funeral director and find out what he or she recommends, or just create your own private service in somebody's home. You might want to create a special place that will have the symbolism of a gravesite or altar.

Ken said the following:

> We haven't found Rowan's body yet, but we did finally have a memorial service, and my parents and I built a memorial for her in our garden. It has a bench and we often sit there—we talk to her, cry for her, it gives us some kind of anchor, and hope, too.

By approaching them with creativity, you will bring life into these sorrowful rituals and occasions. They are painful— nonetheless, you will have to attend to them as best you can.

Community Organizations and Memorials

SOME SURVIVORS CREATE memorials and foundations that will serve their community as well as honor a loved one. Deborah Spungen started Families of Murder Victims after her daughter, Nancy, was murdered. The organization serves the families of murder victims with counseling and programs designed to help support them, both in their private life and through the legal system.

Another well-known example is the national organization, Mothers Against Drunk Drivers, MADD. MADD was established by a group of women in California who were outraged after a teenage girl was killed by a repeat-offender drunk driver. Before MADD was started, little attention was paid to drunk drivers and the awful damage they do. This remarkable organization has changed the way we view drunk driving, lobbying for laws that affect penalties for driving while impaired, and raised national awareness of the crime.

Parents of Murdered Children was started by Charlotte and Bob Hullinger after their daughter Lisa was murdered. POMC helps families face the legal system, from investigations through parole hearings. While this organization provides resources and support for parents who have lost a child, it is an excellent resource for anyone who has survived the violent death of a loved one. POMC's work not only is a testimony to all of us who have suffered, but it is also proof that it is possible to bring something good out of the violent acts we have endured.

Of course, creating an organization takes a significant amount of time and energy—and is something many people may not want to do even at the best of times. You may not want to or be able to do so much work. But you might wish to create a more modest memorial within your community. This can be as simple as what Bette did:

> I wanted to do something in my husband's name and so I sponsored a Little League team, something which Bob loved to coach while he was alive. It didn't cost much to do it and it made me feel really good to see the kids enjoying themselves—we called the team Bob's Boys in his honor.

The Franciscan University dedicated their new playing field collectively to Aaron and Brian and any of their alumni who have died. They called it Memorial Field; it was a beautiful thing to do to honor not only Aaron and Brian but everyone else who has passed on.

Rachel Muha, Brian's mother, holds a golf outing every year on Brian's birthday. The proceeds are used for scholarships to Franciscan university, which are given to worthy young students. The golf outing has grown over the years, and will continue to grow in the future.

A Creative Life

THE CREATIVE LIFE is not just about what you do, but who you are. So while you are finding ways to use this energy in your life, remember that just taking a breath and being part of life is a creative act. As Krista tells us,

> I try to remember that creativity is in everything I do. Instead of seeing death and destruction everywhere as I often do, I also see life all around me, living and breathing, and it's good. I try to be part of that.

Your life is a creative work in progress, like your coral reef. Write about it, create a poem, paint it, draw it, build it, move to it, play music, play a sport, help the needy, throw a birthday party, visit your loved one on a sunny day and bring flowers, give something your loved one loved away to someone else who will also love it, or create a new tradition or a memorial in that person's honor. Every act is evidence that you are alive and a new world to which you can and should belong, awaits you.

The New World

EMERGING POSSIBILITIES

S TAGE 7 IS the last stage of our journey together. It is by no means the end, but it does signal a new development. This stage helps you to step out of the deep onto the shore, and rebuild a new life.

A reminder here: you will set your own pace during your journey. The guidelines I give here are from both my experience and that of others, but you may find that you move through it faster or slower than we did.

The stages interweave with each other, even though certain tasks are distinct to each one. For example, you read in stage 1 about the ways you can tell your story, but you will continue to tell it throughout all the stages. While you may have learned how to ride the waves in stage 4, you may continue to grieve in one form or another throughout your life.

There are, however, milestones, such as getting through the first birthdays, holidays, and anniversaries. Stage 7 takes place after the intense waves have subsided; you will have practiced the three principles to help you move out of the deep and are ready to face the new world. For myself and many others I have spoken with, this took place between the second and fourth year.

That is not to say you won't think or even look forward to the future before you reach the seventh stage. For example, while you may know intellectually even in the first year that the future will hold possibilities and you will rebuild, emotionally you will probably be far too absorbed in the trauma to actually believe it or make it happen in your life. Grief takes time, especially this kind of grief—it will naturally evolve and you must let the journey takes its course.

Nonetheless, if you are reading this and are in the beginning stages, do read this chapter and recognize that, while you may not be here yet, you will be in time, and that, in itself, gives you possibilities for the future.

When you do feel like you are moving forward, you will see that pieces of your former life have survived with you. They are like pieces of driftwood that have battled the waves alongside you, and with which you will rebuild your life.

There is no possible way you can re-create your life the way it was prior to the violent event. That would be to deny the power and magnitude of the trauma that started your journey. Instead, you will rebuild a world that will be an integration of what once was, what it is now, and the possibilities the future. A vital part of this stage is acknowledging and engaging in the future, rather than remaining rooted in your loss. Said Valerie:

> After Devon was murdered, there were no possibilities. Everything was about his death. My world was full of only that; possibilities belonged to other people who still had their child. Not me, I felt like I lost the future when he died.

Violence takes the future and destroys it—but that is only part of the story. The spirit of stage 7 encourages you to take back the future and make it yours again. You must pick up the pieces of your life and put them back together, especially in the following areas:

+ Self
+ Relationships
+ Home
+ Career
+ World

The Driftwood Exercise that follows is designed to help you step onto the new shore and imagine picking up the pieces that you find there.

Find a comfortable place, and plan to spend about fifteen to thirty minutes in private, undisturbed. Place your feet on the floor and put your hands on your lap. Read the following exercise three times and then allow yourself to visualize it.

Begin by taking a nice deep, but gentle, breath. Again. Now, take five breaths and count out loud starting with the number five and going backward until you get to one. Relax your neck, shoulders, arms, belly, legs, and feet. Imagine the tensions floating down to your feet and out to the floor. Quiet your mind and just continue to breathe—like a nice warm breeze coming through your body.

Now, I want you to imagine swimming past your coral reef, coming to the surface, and stepping out of the water onto the shore. Take a moment to feel the ground beneath your feet; it has been a while since you have been on firm ground.

This place is very much like the shore you first started from, yet it is a new part of the world. It is your world now. Take a moment and allow yourself to feel grounded and comfortable, even secure here.

Then look around and notice that you see pieces of driftwood all around you. When you look closer, you see that they are the pieces of the old world that came with you on your journey. You are surprised because you had forgotten about some of them.

Walk along the beach and begin picking up the pieces, and examine them. You understand that you will use these things to help you rebuild your life in this new world. This is the task ahead of you—to rebuild and start again. Realize that you never really stopped; this is just another part of your journey.

Allow yourself to be hopeful again, and maybe even excited, and allow yourself to be filled with possibilities—things you haven't thought about in a long time.

All of the things you find are yours to use as you wish. You will rebuild and the future will come—and it will hold good things for you.

Come out of this exercise holding on to the idea of rebuilding.

After your have done this exercise, you may feel a combination of sadness, hope, and maybe even excitement. This is the way it often is when survivors enter the new world. They are sad and happy, fearful and brave, hopeful yet doubtful.

With this exercise in mind, move on to each of the following areas and see where you retrieve some of the pieces from the past, as you also imagine the possibilities for the future.

Self

WHEN YOU COME out of the deep and look at yourself, you may be surprised by how much you have changed during your journey of grief and suffering. You might not even recognize the person staring back at you in the mirror, you've changed so much. As Linda, whose partner, Bill, was killed, explained,

> In the first two years, I couldn't recognize myself in the mirror. She seemed like someone I didn't know. After I started seriously generating creativity, I started to feel alive again. I wanted to change what I saw, I wanted myself back, and I started taking better care of myself.

Many things change during grief; some people may lose or gain weight, age prematurely, or develop constant fatigue. You may not recognize your physical self. You may feel battered and exhausted, disconnected from yourself. You may have neglected aspects of yourself, such as diet, clothing, even hygiene. Perhaps you have even allowed yourself to slip into an unhealthy dependency, such as the habitual use of sleeping pills.

Often, during this stage, survivors have to make a concentrated decision to take better care of themselves, to pay attention to diet and fitness. Perhaps self-care can be as simple as getting a new hairstyle or buying a new shirt or pair of shoes. It may seem almost laughable—how can these window-dressings really help? But remember, windows help us look outside.

The deeper part of self-care is looking at yourself and realizing that you are alive and that, since you are, you must now decide how you will live. Will you destroy your health by unhealthy habits? Or will you consciously take care of yourself and live again?

Rita realized this profound truth:

> After Don was killed, I started drinking more and taking pills for anxiety. I was out of it for a long time, but actually thought I was coping. I had to take a look at what was happening—I wanted myself back again. I quit drinking and got rid of the pills. I decided I wanted to live—not slowly kill myself.

When the violent act was committed, your life was shattered, pieces of it went flying—and the consequence of that is a disconnection with self. Your private and public selves may have felt out of touch with each other, but now you are coming back together within one body.

Krista told me what it felt like:

> After Katy died, I walked, talked, and did "normal" things. But I recall being on autopilot. I disconnected from the outside world, because I was focused on trying to survive what happened and, without knowing it, I disconnected from me because the feelings were so overwhelming. A few years after it happened, I started

feeling more connected and looked back and wondered,
who was that person?

Reconnecting with yourself is an essential part of your journey. Here are some suggestions on how you can embark on this
process:

+ Look in the mirror and see yourself as you are, with all the wear
  and tear.
+ Acknowledge the changes you see.
+ Acknowledge the suffering you have been through.
+ Give yourself credit—you are still standing!
+ Say hello to who you are now.
+ Take a deep breath and accept who you have become.
+ Practice that great quality of compassion on yourself.
+ Realize that how you are feeling now is a result of what
  happened.
+ Promise yourself you will take care of yourself.
+ Tell yourself: "This is a new world now and I am willing to
  rebuild and make changes."
+ Tell yourself (even if you don't feel this way): "It's good to be
  back."

Remember, acknowledging how much you've been through is
important. You are still standing, and this is a testimony to your
strength. Use your journal to write about the changes that have
occurred, and make sure you begin by congratulating yourself for
your courage and stamina.

When you have completed the above exercise, decide which
areas, if any, are ones where you want to make changes. The very
realization of how much you may have been ravaged by the journey
may be sufficient to encourage you to take better care of yourself.

The following exercise pinpoints which physical areas may need
attending to:

Look in the mirror, and take note of the following areas:

+ Hair
+ Skin
+ Weight
+ Posture
+ Muscle tone
+ General health
+ Clothes

Are there things you want to change? Some changes will be easy—clothes, hair, for instance—while some may be more challenging, such as diet, exercise, and medical attention.

Think about changing the easier things first. Maybe you would like to try a different haircut, that reflects who you are now. Maybe your wardrobe needs overhauling and it's time for a new look, something that suits whom you have become.

Don't be supercritical, have fun doing this—ask a friend for feedback on your appearance; even if you feel fairly satisfied, solicit suggestions for how to spruce up a personal style you've always been comfortable with. Ask him or her to go shopping with you and help you pick out something new. Remember, there is an area where change is good! For both men and women, putting on a "costume" of fresh, new clothes or making some other effort toward your physical person, can help drag you out of your despair.

As Andrea said,

> After Ryan's death—I lost me somewhere. I was floating around, not really caring what I ate or wore or did. I thought I was taking care of myself, but I wasn't. When I started this stage, I decided I could change the way I looked; I cut my hair and bought some new clothes. People were surprised but happy I was doing something for myself. I realized then how long it had been.

You may find that the journey has taken its physical toll on you and that, in addition to more cosmetic kinds of changes as discussed above, you need to develop a good program of exercise, nutrition, and medical advice. These things have been important all along in your journey and were discussed in stage 3. Often, however, they need to be reevaluated during stage 7, and changed or supplemented.

Use your resource network to effect the changes you decide to make. If it's exercise, find a health program, go to the gym, or try a personal trainer. Create a schedule—one that is doable— remember steady progress is always more realistic than aiming for perfection.

In the next exercise, consider personal qualities or characteristics that you may have lost and want to get back. Think of them as things about your personality that you liked. They can be things like being:

+ Outgoing
+ Gregarious
+ Reliable
+ Stable
+ Practical
+ Innovative
+ Adventurous
+ Silly
+ Sexy
+ Or any other trait you can think of

To do this exercise, take some quiet time and think about the person you were just before the trauma happened. You can refer back to the notes you made in stage 1, the ones I asked to make about who you were prior to the loss of your loved one. If you didn't write it down then, you can do it now. You want to focus on such questions as: What were you like? How would people describe you? What do you miss about yourself?

This is an important exercise, because remembering who you were will help you gauge what you have become and what you would like to recover about yourself.

Lea told the following story:

> I always considered myself a gregarious, outgoing person until my husband, Dave, was murdered. I lost that part of myself and, for the first year, I stayed in and just didn't feel like seeing or being out with people. I did this exercise and realized I wanted it back again. I started going out more, and what I discovered was I could only do it for short periods of time. But still, I got some of it back and that's fine—I learned to be more balanced than I was before he was killed.

Reconnecting with who you were doesn't mean you will be the same person as before. It means that some of your former characteristics will return, but, as happened with Lea, they will be tempered and changed by what you have experienced.

Determine which qualities on your list are important to you and test them, as did Lea. If you were a person who liked adventure, then try something new, stretching yourself a little, if you have to.

When Aaron was killed, my sense of adventurousness simply disappeared. It did resurface—much later—when I came out of the deep. However, I am aware that, although I again see possibilities and adventures, I am often wary, tired, and sad even while I go forward—the adventure has been tempered by what happened to Aaron. But nonetheless, I have reconnected with that part of myself, and it feels good.

Whichever qualities you possessed and wish to have back, remember that it may take some practice and practical experience to reawaken them. Today, make a decision to try to practice one of your former qualities and bring it back into your life.

For many survivors, some things will have changed for the better. By that I mean, often, we used to be more concerned with what other people thought about us and we tried to please them, forgetting about ourselves. We may have done things we didn't want to do, just to be liked or because we thought we had to. But when we experienced the violent death of someone we loved, we reevaluated our priorities and decided that while we still care what others think, we are now more concerned with how we feel about us, not how they feel about us.

Realize, too, that you will continue to change, throughout your life. I encourage you to be open to the changes you need to make; let go of some of things about yourself that no longer serve you, and enjoy reconnecting with the parts that do.

Relationships

YOUR RELATIONSHIPS MAY have undergone serious alterations and challenges during your journey. You may find that your burden has been too heavy for some of your relationships with friends or family members, and they have changed or ended. After you have moved through some of your early grief, you can begin to look at where you might change your relationships for the better or be open to developing new ones.

RELATIONSHIPS THAT END

Many times people are unable to come with us on our journey of grief. We feel abandoned, and our loneliness and isolation increases. Often, we are angry or surprised when people turn away from us. Andrea had that experience:

> When Ryan committed suicide, I found that some of my friends turned away from me. They could not handle it—and I think they were afraid their teenage children would somehow "catch" it. My sister avoided talking about Ryan, as if he didn't exist or it didn't happen. I felt like she thought that I must have done something wrong. It hurt so much to go through that—it just added to the terrible pain I was already feeling.

Perhaps you have experienced this painful abandonment. It is important to realize that, sadly, not all relationships will survive this extreme level of pain. People are afraid, and they cannot handle the circumstances, so they may step out of your life.

If this has happened to you, recognize that this violent trauma is difficult for many people and often they just don't know what to do. If the relationship is important to you, then I suggest the following:

Talk to the person, tell him or her you know it is difficult, but your relationship is important and you want this person in your life. Open two-way communications with the person—he or she has feelings that also need to be respected. Say you are willing to listen.

However, make sure these relationships are important enough to you to go through this because, as many report when they do this, you may feel you are "taking care" of these people when, in fact, it is you who need the care.

The truth is there are people who will leave. They will not come with you. This will be part of your grief, and, try as you may, there is nothing you can do about that, except to recognize this, too, is part of your grief and go on without them.

REPAIRING OLD RELATIONSHIPS

Many people will stay with you, and for that you will feel grateful. But within these relationships, there will still be challenges.

Relationships patterns that were formed in the aftermath of violence may need to be looked at and changed. The following exercise will help you assess where the problems are. Write down the answers to the following questions:

+ Are there relationships which have become difficult or uncomfortable since the violence?
+ Have patterns developed which are unhealthy? For example, taking care of someone or someone taking care of you—to the detriment of either?

+ Are you engaging in addictive behavior with someone in order
  to escape the pain? (meaning drug, alcohol, or any behavior that
  causes problems)
+ Are you not talking to or arguing with someone, shut down or
  shut off emotionally?
+ Are you blaming someone or holding someone responsible for
  what happened?
+ Are you not moving forward because the other person is still
  grieving and you don't want to leave him or her behind?

If you answered yes to a question, then complete the following
questions.

+ What is the pattern or behavior that bothers you?
+ Why?
+ How do you want it to change?

Here is an example to help you:

When Rita did the exercise, she realized that she and Don's
brother Derek were drinking together to avoid their pain. It was
becoming an unhealthy pattern; although it may have helped in
the beginning, she wanted it to change now. After she completed
the exercise, she spoke to him and said the following:

"Derek, I want to remain friends with you. We have been
through a lot together, and we will always miss Don. But drinking
isn't helping. I want to stop doing it."

Rita and Derek had to change their relationship in order for
it to survive. They were able to, and today their relationship is not
based on escape—but living.

From your list, determine with whom you have the unhealthy
pattern, what that pattern is, and how you want to change it. Jour-
naling can help you put things in perspective. When you are ready,
use the model above from Rita and Derek or the examples below
to help.

Many of us say or do things out of our grief, sadness, and anger that will damage our relationships. We will want to repair them if possible. If this has happened, try to speak to the person—as Diane learned to do:

> When our parents died in the car crash, my brother and I became so close that we depended on each other for everything. We had a huge falling out because I screamed at him that I didn't want to take care of him. I was angry, and it hurt him and drove him away. I didn't want that to happen; I only wanted space.

Diane sat down with Eric and apologized for hurting him. She then was able to talk calmly about how they needed to have their own lives. This didn't mean they wouldn't take care of each other, but they would have to make better boundaries. For example, Diane wanted to be able to go out on her own without worrying about Eric; and Eric wanted to feel like he, too, had a life. They both agreed to try new ways of taking care of each other and changed their relationship.

You might feel that, although you try to communicate, often you are not heard, as in Jill and David's case.

When Jill and David's son, Brendan, was killed, Jill handled her grief by working through it using many of the techniques she had learned. She talked about it and joined a support group. David, on the other hand, did not want to talk about it and, instead, worked more and withdrew, keeping his grief inside. Jill realized the toll this was taking on their relationship. They were growing more distant. She felt she was moving on—and felt guilty because David wasn't.

She had asked David to talk about it many times, but he had refused. Jill respected the fact that it was his right to choose the way he grieved, but realized that it was damaging their relationship. She eventually told David that their relationship was in trouble and explained what she felt, from her point of view, without blame or accusation. David listened and, while he could not make changes overnight, he cared enough about their relationship to consider what she was saying and try to do something about it.

The important thing is to try and reach out to the ones you love, let them know how you feel—and listen to what they have to say. Do the exercises above, which will help you articulate what you are thinking and feeling, so that when you do sit down with the person, you have a clearer idea of what you want to say, why the problem bothers you, and how you would like it to change.

NEW RELATIONSHIPS

Often in new relationships (but in old ones as well) survivors of a loss are afraid to love again because of the possibility of another loss. To open our hearts again is to risk being hurt again. This is a real fear. How can we trust that it won't happen again? Many of us will close ourselves down instead of taking another risk.

Claire told me the following story:

> Before the first year after Jim was murdered was over, people suggested I should start dating! I thought this was so heartless. How could they tell me I had to move on and meet someone else? I wasn't ready—it wasn't until much later that I even considered the possibility of meeting someone. It's been three years and I now feel like I could have another relationship, but no one will ever replace Jim.

The timing and receptivity to new relationships will be entirely up to you. Some of you may meet someone special to help you; while others of you may decide it is too soon. It is your decision to make.

When you decide to enter another relationship, you will take a risk—that is the nature of love. There is no guarantee it will not hurt. In fact, you can bet it will. And yet, you will love again—it is important to open your heart to the possibility of the future and what relationships it will bring to you.

A word about the love you have for the one you lost. You may think that love is gone, but isn't it more true to say that love endures even when the person is no longer with you? Your task is to find a new relationship with your loved one, one that survives death.

The day of Aaron's funeral, I felt the cord that connected Aaron and me hanging there; I have searched for a connection with him ever since. I have had to find Aaron in my life again. The cord has stretched far and wide. I have seen him in the people I love and felt him in the beauty of nature, the evening star, or the vast open ocean.

There is a verse from the the Song of Songs, in the Old Testament, that gives me solace and strength:

> Set me like a seal on your heart
> Like a seal on your arm
> For love is strong as death
> The flash of it is a flash of fire
> Love no flood can quench
> No torrents drown

This beautiful song is a love story for all of us. Your love for the one you lost is as strong as death and no torrent can drown it, even though you yourself were almost lost in an ocean of grief. You bring that love along with you into the new world, into whatever you do, and wherever you go.

Home

I TRULY BELIEVE in the expression, "Home is where the heart is." So it makes sense that when we experience a trauma, we will often feel that since our hearts are broken, our homes are, too. It's difficult to care about the dishes, laundry, and tidiness when it's a challenge to just get through the day.

Right before Aaron was murdered, I had moved into a small house not far from where my mother lived. At the time of his death, some items were still unpacked. In the months that followed, I had no interest in my home, which was unusual. The funny thing was, I didn't realize it at the time. I did unpack some things, but I was just going through the motions. There was a strange, random quality to these actions: I put objects in odd places or forgetfully left others in the boxes.

It wasn't until several years later, when I moved again, that I began to find things I had put away. I wondered how I could have ignored them. When I started discovering these things, I experienced excitement and joy to see them again—as if they had been lost at sea. It wasn't they; it was I who had been lost.

Try the following exercise:

+ Look around at your environment.
+ Are you happy with it?
+ Do things need to be changed?
+ What would you change?

You may find that certain areas need special attention and, in fact, an urgent feeling to perform "spring cleaning" can help you discharge energy and take control when life feels as if it has spiraled away from you. The following can help:

+ Taking inventory of closets and drawers
+ Making repairs
+ Clearing out basements and garages
+ Going through all paperwork, magazines, and newspapers
+ Getting rid of what you no longer use
+ Finding a special place to save the things that are precious

✦ Redecorating (from painting and wallpapering, to maybe simply putting up a new picture on the wall or investing in a new throw rug or lamp)
✦ Looking for new furniture

You can create new energy in your house and make it a home that reflects this new world you are in. Many people have told me they are amazed at what they have accumulated during the journey, and how much lighter they feel when they go through closets and drawers, discarding what they no longer feel they need in their lives.

Mary told me that after Amy died, she didn't care at all about her house. Several years later, however, she decided to paint the walls pastel colors, fresh and new. They were colors that made her feel peaceful, cheery, and more hopeful about the future than she had been since Amy's death.

You may even want to move to a new house or a new neighborhood. This is another way to begin again, blending what you have now, the things you will add, and the old, precious pieces you decide to keep with you.

If it has been a long time since you really felt at home in your house, ask yourself what you can do right now to make it different. Try the following: Move your favorite chair. It doesn't have to be much, just enough to get a different angle or view. If you can, move it in front of a window. Now sit in the chair and experience the new view. Think about other things you might like to do to make your home more comfortable. Is there a possibility that you can change the way you feel about your home?

Finally, is there something you can choose for your home that will symbolize your journey? It can be a picture of a seascape or person walking on the beach. It can be a statue or small object that reminds you of what you have been through. Make this symbol a part of your home and recognize that this is where you live and that it is a new beginning, a good place to be.

Career

AFTER YOUR TRAUMA, it is almost inevitable that you may experience changes in your work life. In fact, it is not uncommon for survivors to quit their job or be unable to work for a while. On the other hand, many will throw themselves into their work, as Richard did immediately after Susan's death; for him, work was a means of escape, an immersion in an environment and in activities that held little or no direct associations with his wife.

Often, men tell me that is what they do. They find that, because they have a difficult time talking about their feelings, working is at least something gives them a sense of purpose and control. Many women feel this way as well: while we are working, we can escape the pain, if only for the day. Because this stage represents new possibilities, I suggest that you look at what you are doing for work— your actual job, but also your profession—and evaluate whether it still fits into the life you wish to have for yourself or whether your experience has changed what you would like to do.

One of the positive things that comes out of suffering is how it shapes our view of what we want to do in the world. Many survivors report that they want to use their experience to help others. This transformation of suffering into a gift to give to others is a remarkable human quality—much like creativity.

You may find that you want to change careers entirely or take a different direction in the one you already have. For example, Keisha, who was raped, decided to become an advocate for women. She was in law school at the time of her rape. After she took a sabbatical, she finished her degree and represented women who had been raped or experienced domestic abuse.

She said:

> When I started law school, I pictured myself in a
> fancy office doing great corporate work. My experience
> changed that picture. I found a purpose in my life and
> a way of transforming what happened into something

I could use to help others. In the beginning, right after
it happened, though, I wanted to die, and thought
I would. I had no idea I would end up doing what I
do now.

Mary started a day-care center in honor of her daughter, Amy.
She told me that nurturing and caring for children made her feel as
though she was making a difference in their young lives. It helped
her, she said, more than it helped them.

We often read how people transform tragedy into something
that serves others in a very public way. In the last chapter, you read
about survivors who started organizations that will help others who
need to deal with the kind of tragedy they experienced, or to advocate
for changes that could prevent future trauma for others.

There are many ways you can bring the transformative quality
of your suffering to others, either publicly or privately. You can help
stem the wave of violence by volunteering in your community:

+ Become a mentor for at risk youth.
+ Volunteer at community programs for at-risk kids.
+ Coach a sports team.
+ Volunteer for organizations that help people, like Big Brothers/
  Sisters or Boy/Girl Scouts.
+ Help others learn how to read in literacy programs.
+ Volunteer or train to assist victim's advocate programs.

If you want to help others from a more public perspective, you
may consider the following:

+ Form a local chapter of an existing organization, such as
  PoMC.
+ Form an organization that helps others.
+ Form a foundation, in your loved one's name, that helps
  others.
+ Volunteer for any civic organization that helps survivors.

You can also volunteer at your church, temple, or mosque, and assist with any of their programs, from working at a soup kitchen to visiting the sick or elderly. Your acts of service need not relate specifically to the nature of your loss.

If you are thinking of changing careers and want your experience with your loss to inform what you choose, consider the following helping professions:

+ Social work
+ Counseling
+ Medicine
+ Addictions counseling
+ Rape counseling
+ Suicide prevention
+ Nursing
+ Law
+ Writing or public speaking
+ Victims advocate work

Approach such changes step by step. First, consider the lists above and determine which of these appeal to you. Then look into what it would take to accomplish it. For example, if you want to become a social worker, start looking at programs in your area that offer degrees. Read want ads to gain some perspective of what kinds of public or private organizations in your area might professionally employ you, what their job descriptions (duties, hours, and so on) typically consist of, and what the salary range is for the positions you have in mind. Then consider your potential qualifications, and your willingness to take the time and make the investment toward such a career move, and determine whether it is something you want to proceed with. Do not make hasty decisions, but consider carefully the challenges you will face.

You can also speak to someone who is already doing what you are considering; ask if you can talk to them about their experience, and if they can advise you—like a mentor. After all, they can share with you how they got to where they are, which can help and inspire you, as well as give you some sense of whether you might not want to enter their profession after all.

Remember there are many ways to help others without changing your career. You will want to consider realistically the cost, time, and energy such changes will require before you plunge into anything for which you do not have at least some related professional experience to build upon.

Many people may want to change careers but to do something very different than anything associated with their trauma. For example, Sarah, whose sister, Mia, was raped and murdered said:

> I decided I wanted to bring beauty into the world. I became a florist. I loved making flower arrangements for people, weddings, even funerals. I wanted to bring color and beauty and fragrance so they could celebrate. When I knew it was a funeral, I could relate and make something so lovely, it would help them forget their grief for a moment.

While many of us will use our experience to help others privately and publicly, we will all have the most important job of all, and that is to survive the violence and live again. This means helping your own family first—and, more than likely, this is something that will continue throughout your lives together.

So, no matter which stage you are in or what you would like to do—first things first—take care of yourself and your family, even if it means sticking with the job you have so you will provide for them . . . or taking time off to spend more time with them.

Loyalty

LOYALTY IS AN admirable, but somewhat confusing quality—one with which survivors have a tumultuous relationship. Often, we think that to desire to move forward is to be disloyal to the one we love. We feel guilty about a future that does not include the person—or the possibility that things can and will go on without him or her. After, all, how can we be happy when such an awful thing happened?

This is particularly true for us who have lost someone to violence. The fact that our loved one suffered so brutally, and was taken from us so abruptly, compounds our grief and our ability to move forward. It is as though the act of violence keeps us glued to it. We cannot separate ourselves; we are stuck, living and reliving the event in our daily lives. Does this sound dramatic? Think about it: since your own tragedy happened, hasn't it occupied most of your thoughts, even though you seemed to be doing something else?

You may feel as if, if you move on, you will leave your loved one behind. Your sense of loyalty says you must live with this person, wherever he or she may be, and the suddenness of the event keeps you rooted in your loved one's horrible last moments. Your love causes you to want to be with him or her, and your grief keeps you there. The thought of moving on is not only repugnant to you, but seems impossible.

To blithely say you *have* moved on is like saying you are healed, which you are not. This speaks to the notion of "closure." Many survivors (myself included) find these concepts insensitive and an affront to what has happened.

Perhaps that is why your grief is a grief like no other. There simply is no closure. It is never over—you are never healed. It is more true to say that you *are* moving on, as an ever-changing process; that you are putting your life back together again in new ways, but that these ways are laced through with tender memories of your loved one, not just the violent act that you have been submerged in for so long. You become strong in the places that violence has broken you, and yet at the same time recognize how fragile and precious you and all of life are. You are now able have thoughts and feelings about your loved one that contain pleasure, serenity, perhaps even humor, rather than dread, at least most of the time.

You are not disloyal to the dead when you celebrate new life within your own self or the world. Quite the contrary, you will take your loved one along within you no matter where you go or what you do. You are *both* moving forward.

My Story

IN 2003, THINGS started to shift for me. Finally, I began to glimpse the other side of the shore and think of life's possibilities again. Slowly, almost imperceptibly, I felt better. That doesn't mean I didn't cry or mourn, but acceptance and gratitude began to shape my life.

Since I realized that I wasn't going to die of grief and that I couldn't stay in the deep forever, what did the future hold for me? I imagined that I might do something different with my life. I began to anticipate that happiness could be mine again. I felt stronger, less afraid, and certainly more hopeful than I had felt in a long time.

During this time, I had a dream. I tell you this because it is important, but I also know that I often felt sad when others told me about their dreams, while I had none of Aaron. This story is a gift and I want to share it with you, in hopes that it will inspire you.

I dreamed that Aaron and I were driving in my car. He was young, maybe ten or twelve. We were going to see him in his school play, as we had done in real life. We arrived, and I sat in the audience watching him onstage. Suddenly, the stage turned iridescent, electric blue and gold. It began to undulate, radiating light in different shapes. Aaron held his arm out and pointing his finger, touched the blue. He became part of it, and pulsing light radiated from him until he was absorbed in it. I watched the light and was stunned by its beauty. It was unlike anything I had ever seen. Aaron was showing me what it was like where he was! I was enraptured. He told me about love, about God, and the power of life to continue, even after death. I understood what he was saying.

I awoke, full of an indescribable feeling, like joy, but something much more. I couldn't remember anything he told me, but I do remember what I had seen. It was a gift. The power I saw in that dream was extraordinary; it gave me strength and courage to go on.

I grew stronger over time, and, looking back, I see that with each month's and year's passage, I changed. I didn't feel as lost or alone. The memories of my old life started to form the foundations of the new. I remembered who I was before this all happened. I was a person who enjoyed the world, liked adventure, and had an optimistic view of life. As I felt these things return, I felt them tempered by the absolute knowledge that things can change in a moment, and to respect what I had in the present.

On Thanksgiving 2004, my children and I celebrated together as we always did. We sat at the table with Aaron's chair close by. The space felt smaller, more natural. We had knit together another form of our family; the three of us and Aaron, too. A few days later, when Anna and Michael left, I sat and cried for Aaron. It was a soft crying, missing him, wishing he was there; but with more acceptance.

On December 1, 2004, a few days after Thanksgiving, I received a call from Teresa Laman, the victim's advocate I told you about, in the Steubenville district attorney's office. She was calling to tell me that the Supreme Court of Ohio vacated both the death penalty and the murder conviction in the case of Terrell Yarbrough.

They ruled that the trial should have taken place in Pennsylvania, where the bodies of Aaron and Brian were found. To my incredible shock and horror, I was told that the case would have to be retried in Pennsylvania—otherwise Terrell would be convicted of burglary, kidnapping, and assault—but not murder.

This, too, is why our grief is a grief like no other. Just when I thought I had at least some degree of closure and a measure of justice, my family and I are being forced to endure the whole thing all over again.

My grief and terror returned. However, I have learned how to live with these things. I have tried to put it out of my mind until it actually happens and will face it again when it does. We are still awaiting word of the new trial date.

In the meantime, I try to practice some form of acceptance, using the tools I have shared with you in this book. This is not to say that I do not grieve for Aaron; not a day goes by that I do not think of him and wish this awful thing had never happened. There are days when I am filled with anger and despair and when the undertow of grief drags me toward the deep again. Sometimes, I have to use everything I know and have told you about, to come out. Sometimes, I still feel like giving up—and then I surrender to my sadness and realize this is the nature of our grief. Once I accept that, it passes and life goes on. . . .

Your Story

THE FIRST STAGE of your journey focused on shaping your own, unique story into something manageable. You have done that, and you have learned to carry it across the waters with you.

But what happens to it now that you are on the shores of the new world? Your story will always be a part of you and will continue to change throughout the coming years. There will be times when you will feel it digging into your shoulders or pressing into your belly—sometimes, when you least expect it.

As time passes, however, you may be able to forget it is there. But it hasn't disappeared. It becomes woven into the new life you build; it is in the warp and weave of everything you do, inseparable from the person you have become.

You will meet people and do things, and no one will know your loved one. You may not tell your story very often. People may not even know it exists. Yet, it will live in your heart along with that moment when everything changed in that one phone call, discovery, or act of witness.

You will be glad you kept a record of the story for others and, sometimes, on a gray day, you will take it out and honor it and cry over it. Then you will put it away, tuck it back into your heart, and go forward.

In time, you will realize that what once was a crushing burden is something you now have power over. You can now think new thoughts, and move about freely your new life, neither of which seemed possible not too long ago.

Remember that your story is a love story, and is stronger than death. This song of love overshadows the story your journey began with—and is one that will last for a lifetime.

A Whole Life

WHAT GIFT CAN you give your loved one who is always with you? Live the best life you can—every day a new beginning. *You* are still alive, for better or worse, and have the greatest of the human freedoms, the freedom to choose how you will live.

There's still time for you to live, time for you to enjoy—time to build yourself a whole life, one that honors and embraces, rather than only mourns, your loved one.

I am reminded of the Jewish prayer for Yom Kippur, which says it best:

> It is hard to sing of oneness when our world is not complete, when those who once brought wholeness to our life have gone, and nothing but memory can fill the emptiness their passing leaves behind.
>
> But memory can tell us only what we were, in company with those we loved; it cannot help us find what each of us, alone, must now become. Yet no one is really alone: those who live no more echo still within our thoughts and words, and what they did is part of what we have become. We do best homage to our dead when we live our lives most fully, even in the shadow of our loss.

RESOURCES

Trauma Therapies, Community Organizations, and Support Groups

LOOK THROUGH YOUR local yellow pages or search on the Web for resources for trauma counselors and trauma/bereavement groups. Use such keywords as "trauma victim," "bereavement," "crisis counseling," "community support," "suicide," "murder victim."

Here are a few that may help:

American Counseling Association (ACA)
www.counseling.org
Offers "Crisis Fact Sheets" to help children and adults cope with uncertain times and other emotional crises. From the home page, click on Consumers.

American Academy of Child and Adolescent Psychiatry (AACAP)
www.aacap.org/publications/factsfam/disaster.htm
Gives tips that help children cope after a disaster such as an earthquake, hurricane, tornado, fire, flood, or following violent acts.

National Mental Health and Education Center
www.naspcenter.org/safe_schools/coping.html
Provides information on reactions to disaster, stages of reactions to loss, and common stress symptoms.

National Mental Health Association
www.nmha.org/reassurance/children.cfm
Helps children cope with loss, PTSD, and disaster-related anxiety.

National Center for Post-Traumatic Stress Disorder
www.ncptsd.org/publications/disaster/index.html
Offers a 160-page guidebook in .html or .pdf formats that includes stress reactions, helping survivors, helping helpers, helping organizations, and team and program development.

American Psychological Association
telephone: 800-964-2000
www.apahelpcenter.org

United Way
www.211.org

www.griefnet.org
An Internet community of people dealing with grief, death, and major loss.

Parents of Murdered Children
www.pomc.com

Compassionate Friends
www.compassionatefriends.org

Families of Murder Victims
www.avpphila.org

National Organization of Victims Assistance
www.trynova.org

Mothers against Drunk Drivers (MADD)
www.madd.org

National Center for Victims of Crime
www.ncvc.org

Families & Friends of Violent Crime Victims
www.fnfvcv.org

National Survivors of Suicide Day
www.afsp.org/survivor/conference

Surviving Suicide
www.survivingsuicide.com

The Center for Victims
telephone: 412-346-7555
www.cwc.org

Note: If you are trying to find victims services in your area, call your district attorney's office and ask if they have a victim's services or advocate office. If they do not, ask them what assistance is available in your area.

HYPNOTHERAPY

American Association of Professional Hypnotherapists
www.aaph.org

The Milton H. Erickson Institute
www.ericksonfoundation.org/institutes/institut.htm

ALTERNATIVE OR HOLISTIC
APPROACHES TO CARE

An alternative approach to mental health care is one that emphasizes the interrelationship between mind, body, and spirit. Although some alternative approaches have a long history, many remain controversial. The National Center for Complementary and Alternative Medicine at the National Institutes of Health was created in 1992 to help evaluate alternative methods of treatment and to integrate those that are effective into mainstream health-care practice. It is crucial, however, to consult with your health-care providers about the approaches you are using to achieve mental wellness.

Self-help

Many people find that self-help groups are an invaluable resource for recovery and for empowerment. Self-help generally refers to groups or meetings that:

+ Involve people who have similar needs
+ Are facilitated by a consumer, survivor, or other layperson
+ Assist people to deal with a "life-disrupting" event, such as a death, abuse, serious accident, addiction, or diagnosis of a physical, emotional, or mental disability, for oneself or a relative
+ Are operated on an informal, free-of-charge, and nonprofit basis
+ Provide support and education
+ Are voluntary, anonymous, and confidential

Diet and Nutrition

Adjusting both diet and nutrition may help some people with mental illnesses manage their symptoms and promote recovery. For example, research suggests that eliminating milk and wheat products can reduce the severity of symptoms for some people who have schizophrenia and some children with autism. Similarly, some holistic/natural physicians use herbal treatments, B-complex vitamins, riboflavin, magnesium, and thiamine to treat anxiety, autism, depression, drug-induced psychoses, and hyperactivity.

Pastoral Counseling

Some people prefer to seek help for mental health problems from their pastor, rabbi, or priest, rather than from therapists who are not affiliated with a religious community. Counselors working within traditional faith communities increasingly are recognizing the need to incorporate psychotherapy and/or medication, along with prayer and spirituality, to effectively help some people with mental disorders.

Expressive Therapies

Art Therapy: Drawing, painting, and sculpting help many people to reconcile inner conflicts, release deeply repressed emotions, and foster self-awareness, as well as personal growth. Some mental health providers use art therapy as both a diagnostic tool and as a way to help treat disorders such as depression, abuse-related trauma, and schizophrenia. You may be able to find a therapist in your area who has received special training and certification in art therapy.

Dance/Movement Therapy: Some people find that their spirits soar when they let their feet fly. Others—particularly those who prefer more structure or who feel they have two left feet—gain the same sense of release and inner peace from the Eastern martial arts, such as Aikido and Tai Chi. Those who are recovering from physical, sexual, or emotional abuse may find these techniques especially helpful for gaining a sense of ease with their own bodies.

The underlying premise to dance/movement therapy is that it can help a person integrate the emotional, physical, and cognitive facets of "self."

Music/Sound Therapy: It is no coincidence that many people turn on soothing music to relax or snazzy tunes to help feel upbeat. Research suggests that music stimulates the body's natural "feel-good" chemicals (opiates and endorphins). This stimulation results in improved blood flow, blood pressure, pulse rate, breathing, and posture changes. Music or sound therapy has been used to treat stress, grief, depression, schizophrenia, and autism in children, and to diagnose mental health needs.

Culturally Based Healing Arts

Traditional Chinese and Japanese medicine (such as acupuncture, shiatsu, and reiki), Indian systems of health care (such as Ayurveda and yoga), and Native American healing practices (such as the Sweat Lodge and Talking Circles) all incorporate the beliefs that:

+ Wellness is a state of balance between the spiritual, physical, and mental/emotional "selves."
+ An imbalance of forces within the body is the cause of illness.
+ Herbal/natural remedies, combined with sound nutrition, exercise, and meditation/prayer, will correct this imbalance.

Acupuncture: The Chinese practice of inserting needles into the body at specific points manipulates the body's flow of energy to balance the endocrine system. This manipulation regulates functions such as heart rate, body temperature, and respiration, as well as sleep patterns and emotional changes. Acupuncture has been used in clinics to assist people with substance abuse disorders through detoxification; to relieve stress and anxiety; to treat attention deficit and hyperactivity disorder in children; to reduce symptoms of depression; and to help people with physical ailments.

Ayurveda: Ayurvedic medicine is described as "knowledge of how to live." It incorporates an individualized regimen—such as diet, meditation, herbal preparations, and other techniques—to treat a variety of conditions, including depression, to facilitate lifestyle changes and to teach people how to release stress and tension through yoga or transcendental meditation.

Yoga/meditation: Practitioners of this ancient Indian system of health care use breathing exercises, posture, stretches, and meditation to balance the body's energy centers. Yoga is used in combination with other treatment for depression, anxiety, and stress-related disorders.

Native American traditional practices: Ceremonial dances, chants, and cleansing rituals are part of Indian Health Service programs to heal depression, stress, trauma (including those related to physical and sexual abuse), and substance abuse.

Relaxation and Stress-Reduction Techniques
Biofeedback: Learning to control muscle tension and "involuntary" body functioning, such as heart rate and skin temperature, can be a path to mastering one's fears. It is used in combination with, or as an alternative to, medication to treat disorders such as anxiety, panic, and phobias. For example, a person can learn to "retrain" his or her breathing habits in stressful situations to induce relaxation and decrease hyperventilation. Some preliminary research indicates it may offer an additional tool for treating schizophrenia and depression.

Guided Imagery or Visualization: This process involves going into a state of deep relaxation and creating a mental image of recovery and wellness. Physicians, nurses, and mental health providers occasionally use this approach to treat alcohol and drug addictions, depression, panic disorders, phobias, and stress.

Massage therapy: The underlying principle of this approach is that rubbing, kneading, brushing, and tapping a person's muscles can help release tension and pent emotions. It has been used to treat trauma-related depression and stress. A highly unregulated industry, certification for massage therapy varies widely from state to state. Some states have strict guidelines, while others have none.

American Art Therapy Association, Inc.
1202 Allanson Road
Mundelein, IL 60060-3808
telephone: 847-949-6064/888-290-0878
fax: 847-566-4580
e-mail: info@arttherapy.org
www.arttherapy.org

American Association of Pastoral Counselors
9504-A Lee Highway
Fairfax, VA 22031-2303
telephone: 703-385-6967
fax: 703-352-7725
e-mail: info@aapc.org
www.aapc.org

American Chiropractic Association
1701 Clarendon Boulevard
Arlington, VA 22209
telephone: 800-986-4636
fax: 703-243-2593
www.amerchiro.org

American Dance Therapy Association
2000 Century Plaza, Suite 108
10632 Little Patuxent Parkway
Columbia, MD 21044
telephone: 410-997-4040
fax: 410-997-4048
e-mail: info@adta.org
www.adta.org

American Music Therapy Association
8455 Colesville Rd, Suite 1000
Silver Spring, MD 20910
telephone: 301-589-3300
fax: 301-589-5175
e-mail: info@musictherapy.org
www.musictherapy.org

American Association of Oriental Medicine
5530 Wisconsin Avenue, Suite 1210
Chevy Chase, MD 20815
telephone: 888-500-7999
fax: 301-986-9313
e-mail: info@aaom.org
www.aaom.org

National Empowerment Center
599 Canal Street
Lawrence, MA 01840
telephone: 800-769-3728
fax: 508-681-6426
www.power2u.org

National Mental Health Consumers' Self-Help Clearinghouse
1211 Chestnut Street, Suite 1207
Philadelphia, PA 19107
telephone: 800-553-4539
fax: 215-636-6312
e-mail: info@mhselfhelp.org
www.mhselfhelp.org

International Association of Yoga Therapists
P.O. Box 426
Manton, CA 96059
telephone: 530-474-5700.
fax: 530-474-5704
email: mail@yrec.org
*Now a division of the Yoga Research and Education Center, the
International Association of Yoga Therapists seeks to promote the
field of yoga therapy and publishes an annual journal and tri-annual
newsletter.*

Meditation Resources
You can go to my Web site, www.kathleenohara.com, to find out
about my meditation CD. Or, you can search the Web using the
keywords "meditation classes," or ask your local gym, yoga studio,
or college if they offer such classes.

Somatic Therapies
If you wish to learn more about somatics, the following is an excel-
lent resource: *Bone Breath and Gesture: Practices of Embodiment*, by
Don Hanlon Johnson (Berkeley, California: North Atlantic Books).
This is an outstanding collection of articles by Breathwork specialists
of various kinds, including Ilse Middendorf, Elsa Gindler, Moshe
Feldenkreis, Ida Rolf, Gerda Alexander who invented eutony, and
Thomas Hanna who was so influential in the creation of the field
of somatics.

California Institute of Integral Studies (CIIS)
Somatics Department
1453 Mission Street
San Francisco, CA 94103
telephone: 415-575-6100
www.ciis.edu

Rosen Method: The Berkeley Center
Berkeley, California
telephone: 510-845-6606
fax: 510-845-8114
e-mail: rosenmethod@sbcglobal.net
www.rosenmethod.com/berkschool

Foundation for Human Enrichment
Peter Levine
P.O. Box 1872
Lyons, CO 80540
telephone: 303-823-9524
www.traumahealing.com

Creativity Resources
Scrapbooking: Look in the yellow pages for local resources or go
to these sites:

> www.scapbook.com
> www.luv2scrapbook.com
> www.creatingkeepsakes.com

Crafts: Check out magazines and shops in your area which offer
crafts, and search the Web using the keywords of the craft you
wish to search.

Mask making: Ask your local art colleges if they have classes or consult the Web, using the keyphrase: "mask-making classes." The following Web site is an example of what's available.

www.maskmakersweb.org

Expressive Arts (painting, writing, sculpting): Find local resources by contacting art schools and community organizations. Or, search the Web using the keyphrase "expressive arts," plus the name of the art you wish to inquire about: e.g., painting classes. Or contact:

American Art Therapy Association, Inc.
1202 Allanson Road
Mundelein, IL 60060-3808
telephone: 847-949-6064/888-290-0878
fax: 847-566-4580
e-mail: info@arttherapy.org
www.arttherapy.org

HELP WITH ADDICTIONS

Look in your local yellow pages and on the Web for self-help organizations. Here are some national ones that have local branches:

Alcoholics Anonymous
www.alcoholics-anonymous.org

Gamblers Anonymous
www.gamblersanonymous.org

Narcotics Anonymous
www.na.org

Further Reading

THIS IS ONLY a partial list of good books available to help you. Please visit your bookstore or online provider to learn about others.

Brook, Noel and Pamela D. Blair. *I Wasn't Ready to Say Goodbye: Surviving, Coping and Healing after the Sudden Death of a Loved One.* Belgium, WI: Champion Press, 2002.

Fine, Carla. *No Time to Say Goodbye, Surviving the Suicide of a Loved One.* New York: Doubleday, 1997.

Kushner, Harold S. *When Bad Things Happen to Good People.* New York: Avon, 1981.

Levine, Peter A. *Waking the Tiger, Healing Trauma.* Berkeley, CA: North Atlantic Books, 1997.

Lord, Janice Harris: *No Time for Goodbyes: Coping with Sorrow, Anger and Injustice after a Tragic Death.* Oxnard, CA: Pathfinder Publications, 2002.

McCracken, Anne and Mary Semel. *A Broken Heart Still Beats— After Your Child Dies.* Center City, MN: Hazelden, 1998.

Naparstek, Belleruth. *Invisible Heroes—Survivors of Trauma and How They Heal.* New York: Bantam Dell, 2004.

Rooks, Diane. *Spinning Gold out of Straw, How Stories Heal.* St. Augustine, FL: Salt Run Press, 2001.

Rosof, Barbara D. *The Worst Loss, How Families Heal from the Death of a Child.* New York: Henry Holt & Company, 1994.

Sebold, Alice: *The Lovely Bones.* New York: Little, Brown and Company, 2002.

Sogyal Rinpoche. *The Tibetan Book of Living and Dying.* New York: HarperCollins Publishers, 1992.

Spungen, Deborah. *And I Don't Want to Live this Life: A Mother's Story of Her Daughter's Murder.* New York: Ballantine Books, 1996.

Spungen, Deborah. *Homicide: The Hidden Victims: A Resource for Professionals*. Thousand Oaks, CA: Sage Publications, 1997.

Williams, Mary Beth and Soili Poijula. *The PTSD Workbook*. Oakland, CA: New Harbinger Publications, 2002.

BOOKS TO HELP CHILDREN COPE WITH GRIEF

Mundy, Michaelene and R. W. Alley. *Sad Isn't Bad: A Good-Grief Guidebook for Kids Dealing with Loss*. Abbey Press, 1998. (for kids ages 4–8)

Silverman, Janice. *Help Me Say Goodbye: Activities for Helping Kids Cope when a Special Person Dies*. Minneapolis: Fairview Press, 1999. (art therapy, for kids ages 4–8)

Thomas, Pat and Lesley Harker. *I Miss You: A First Look at Death*. Hauppage, NY: Barron's Educational Series, 2001. (for kids ages 4–8)

BOOKS TO HELP YOU TELL
YOUR CHILDREN ABOUT DEATH

Dougy Center for Grieving Children. *35 Ways to Help a Grieving Child*. Portland, OR: Dougy Center, 1999.

Goldman, Linda. *Breaking the Silence: A Guide to Help Children with Complicated Grief: Suicide, Homicide, AIDS, Violence, and Abuse*. Ann Arbor, MI: Sheridan Books, 2001.

Kroen, William C. and Pamela Espeland. *Helping Children Cope with the Loss of a Loved One: A Guide for Grown-ups*. Minneapolis: Free Spirit Publishing, 1996.

INDEX